CLINT EASTWOOD

ALL-AMERICAN ANTI-HERO

A CRITICAL APPRAISAL OF THE WORLD'S TOP BOX OFFICE STAR AND HIS FILMS BY DAVID DOWNING AND GARY HERMAN

Art Directed by Pearce Marchbank/Designed by Ken Carroll

Omnibus Press

London/New York/Cologne/Sydney

CONTENTS

Photographs courtesy of Universal International, R.K.O., United Artist, Warner Brothers, M.G.M., C.I.C., CBS Television, Camera Press, BBC, BFI.

Many thanks to Cornelia Bach, Janet Scott, and Phil Hardy.

Distributed by Book Sales Limited, 78 Newman Street, London W1P 3LA. Book Sales Pty Limited, 27 Clarendon Street, Artarmon, Sydney, NSW 2064, Australia.

Quick Fox, 33 West 60th Street, New York 10023, New York, U.S.A.

© Copyright 1977 by David Downing and Gary Horman

ISBN 0 86001 412 6. UK Order No. OP 4027 E. US Order No. 0309 9

Printed in England by Lowe & Brydone Printers Limited, Thetford, Norfolk

DEDICATION

Owen Wister's western novel, 'The Virginian', has been filmed three times under that name: in 1914 with Dustin Farnum in the title role, in 1930 with Gary Cooper and in 1945 with Joel McCrea. The plot has been borrowed several times. In 1964, Charles Marquis Warren turned this first serious novel of the old West into a TV series.

During one scene in the novel, the hero Trampas, is playing poker with the mysterious and villainous stranger who is known only as the Virginian. Trampas speaks to his opponent:

"Your bet, you son of a bitch."

The Virginian rests his gun on the table and ' in a voice as gentle as ever... sounding like a caress, but drawling a very little more than usual' he says:

"When you call me that, smile."

This book is respectfully dedicated to all those who forgot to smile and all the punks who didn't feel lucky.

CHAPTER 1
JUST THE WAY IT IS (1930-59)

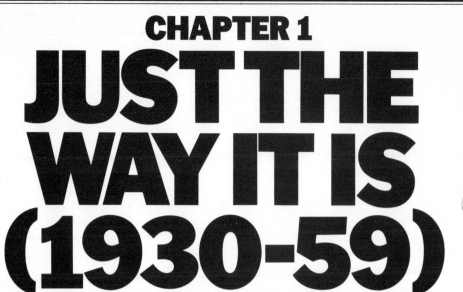

> 'Any actor going into pictures has to have something special. That's what makes a star while a lot of damn good actors are passed by. The public recognises their work as good but they don't run out to see them with their three dollars for a ticket. The public goes to see the stars. I didn't invent those rules – that's just the way it is'
> – Clint Eastwood

EASTWOOD AT THE TIME OF BIT PARTS. FAR LEFT: 'TARANTULA' (1954) IN WHICH HE HAD A MINOR ROLE

A NEW BREED OF HERO

The scene is familiar. Two women, one old, the other young and beautiful, are prisoners of the evil Comancheros. Tied to the backs of the villains' wagon they stumble along, headed for a fate that in this case might really be worse than death. But then, lo and behold, on the skyline he appears, wreathed in the golden sun. It's the hero, tall in the saddle, bearing the twin guns of power and righteousness.

The camera zooms in on the hero, and here is the first shock for anyone who hadn't seen a film for forty years. The hero is unshaven. Not bearded, merely unshaven. He squints the Comancheros straight in the eye, and spews a long stream of tobacco juice onto the ground. This is not the elegance of a Gable or a Flynn. Suddenly he dispenses with his flag of truce and shoots four men dead. This is hardly cricket. A bare minute later the other seven or so nasties are ready for a burial they won't get. As our hero has said earlier in the film, with his usual conciseness — "buzzards gotta eat same as worms". Not surprisingly the heroine and her grandmother, far from rushing to thankfully embrace this all-powerful maniac, just stare aghast at the carnage he has wrought.

This scene from *The Outlaw Josey Wales* is a fairly representative sample of Clint Eastwood, Hollywood superstar of the 1970s.

Certain aspects of movie heroism seem almost eternal. The hero is potent and graceful in action. He wins. He is both surly and gentle, softly-spoken and forceful. Beneath the tough exterior lurks a heavy hint of sentimentality. Like Cooper, Gable, Bogart or Wayne this hero is good-looking in an unconventional way. In some ways he resembles them all. And like each of them he is unique.

But time has also frayed the hero. Unlike Flynn he neither relishes life's battles nor reaps his due reward in the heroine's arms. He is doomed to isolation by the same righteousness that Wayne makes his home. This hero's clothes are not white, his motives are not simple. Issues, like his countenance, are no longer clean-cut. He has been through Bogart's reluctance to get involved, through Brando and Dean's confused rebellion. They have influenced him, but they have not converted him. He is still a hero, one without answers. His victories promise survival, not rewards.

A changing world means a changing film industry; both have transformed our hero. In the 1930s Hollywood wove its diaphanous dreams across a

backcloth of unemployment, poverty and general human degradation. Today the backcloth is not so different, perhaps a little starker, a little closer to home. Why does Hollywood no longer weave its dreams? The answer lies in the development of the industry, its steady decline before the twin threats of television and the post-war European cinema, threats that forced a re-evaluation of what movies would make money, and of what heroes would strike a chord in the public consciousness.

It is no accident that Clint Eastwood's rise to stardom was via exactly these two media, television and the modern European cinema. Having conquered each he could return to Hollywood and become its biggest star for the seventies. With one foot firmly planted in the Hollywood tradition, the other in the shifting sands of the contemporary world. That is why he is the biggest, the top box-office star of the age. Stars like Charlton Heston are traditional stars, those like Jack Nicholson modern stars. Only Eastwood straddles the two categories. Only he can present living issues in the larger-than-life terms of Hollywood.

FROM BIRTH TO BIT-PARTS

Clinton Eastwood junior was born into the Great Depression on 30th May, 1930, in San Francisco. Clinton senior was a cost accountant by training, but depressions are not kind to that profession, and the family travelled around California as he searched for work. Eventually they settled in Oakland, just across the bay from San Francisco, where he had found employment with the Georgia Pacific Company.

Young Clinton went to Oakland Technical High School where his height gave him a definite edge on the basketball court. But he seems to have developed no abiding interests while at school (except possibly swimming) and after graduation he became a lumberjack in Oregon. "I was never an extrovert," he remembers, "but I longed for independence, even though I got along with my parents . . . I didn't know what I really wanted to do". One thing he didn't want to do was to act. An appearance in a school play had cured him of any such dreams.

But the fates had decided otherwise. During the Korean War he was called up, but luckily the Army was more in need of swimming instructors than cannon fodder at that moment, and he was posted to nearby Fort Ord for the duration of his enlistment. One day a Universal film crew decamped at the Fort and the assistant director, noticing Eastwood, told him to come and see him when his two-year stint was over. While still in the army he met actor David Janssen, who also recommended a career in films.

Eastwood was not convinced, and finding that the director had left Universal he decided to go to college, opting for a course in business administration at Los Angeles City College. He took a number of casual jobs during this period — among them petrol pump attending and car delivery driving — and also met and married Maggie Johnson, then a student at Berkeley.

Perhaps it was his marriage that inspired Eastwood to try the movie industry once more. In any event, he went back to Universal to see David Janssen and another army buddy who had become a cameraman. They persuaded a director to give him a screen test. "I had to stand in an office set and just walk around," Eastwood recalls. "They were talking to me off camera trying to get different expressions, but the only expression I could register was one of stark terror." It was enough. "The next day they asked me if I'd be interested in the training programme."

This involved acting classes, riding lessons and playing bit-parts. The contract provided for forty weeks' work a year guaranteed, at a wage of a little over $70 a week. "That seemed like a million dollars to me," says Eastwood now. He was doing well, which was more than could be said for the industry.

BRING ON THE EMPTY STUDIOS

The golden years of Hollywood, as its survivors never tire of telling everybody, were the 1930s. Sound had arrived at the end of the twenties, the first workable colour system at the beginning of the thirties, and a new breed of stars were being groomed for a long line of unprecedentedly successful films. The industry boomed. In 1930 it was dominated by just eight companies — Fox, MGM, Warner Brothers, Paramount, RKO, Columbia, Universal and United Artists. By 1936 these eight themselves dominated financially by America's two greatest banking groups, Morgan and Rockefeller. The vaults bulged; writers, producers, directors and stars lived in platinum palaces of sin, their lives straight out of their own movies. The years passed in an intoxicated haze. Dollars flowed into LA like wine, and the LA wine flowed like water.

But after the war things changed. By the time Clint Eastwood entered the movie business it was well into a long hangover. The rest of the developed world was enjoying the dividends of post-war reconstruction but Hollywood, the fountainhead of ephemera and ever-susceptible to forces beyond its own control, was clearly suffering. In the early forties there had been a space for film reels in the ships and planes that carried America's arms, food, oil and soldiers across the Atlantic. And though this continued after the war, by the early fifties European culture had begun to recover and the United States started to slip from its position as manufacturer of cultural commodities to the world. In a short time many European countries had developed healthy domestic film industries. Hollywood's export markets shrank, money flowed into European investments, and soon the new European movies began to invade the United States.

This threat to Hollywood's well-being demanded a response. Something would have to change. The product emanating from the new European cinema

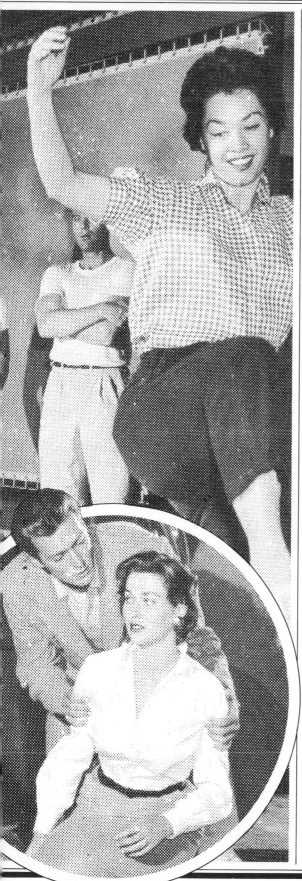

tended to be more adventurous, more innovative. Hollywood too would have to take some risks.

But this it was ill-equipped to do. For one thing there was the natural conservatism of the major studios. Having already coined millions out of proven formulae they were reluctant, and probably unable, to seek out new ones. The great producers who had lived and breathed movies were giving way to neophytes and accountants. The last tycoon had passed away. The new studio bosses juggled figures rather than dreams, and the only dreams that did penetrate their consciousness were the old ones. Their only answer to present and future was a doomed attempt to re-create the glories of the past.

Other factors encouraged this ostrich-like stance, most notably the McCarthyite witch-hunts which

'My father always kept telling me you don't get anything for nothing, and although I rebelled I never rebelled against that'

saw the spectre of International Communism in any socially concerned or unconventional film. Writers, producers, directors and actors were sacked, black-listed or just eased off the payroll almost every other day, and anybody suspected of communist sympathies might as well kiss a movie career goodbye. Even respected and renowned figures — Charlie Chaplin was only the most famous — were caught in the paranoid web of anti-communism, and very few people, with their livelihoods at stake, were inclined to risk investigation or a smear campaign. Hollywood's need might have been for more adventurous films, but in the early fifties the pressure felt by individuals and companies to toe an unadventurous line was more keenly felt.

If Hollywood could not compete with the European cinema in terms of innovation, neither could it compete with television in churning out the old formulas. The new medium offered audiences everything that films could — moving picture, sound, and in the US at least, colour — with the added advantages of lower production costs and greater viewer convenience. On top of that, sponsorship and advertising gave television a built-in financial headstart. Hollywood producers had to raise vast amounts of money to pay for films months before a cent came back to them from the box office. Even then, no studio could ever guarantee success for any particular movie.

Television companies, on the other hand, were in the business of selling advertising. Their shows were short and relatively cheap to produce, advertising was pre-sold so the profitability of each show could

'HELL BENT FOR GLORY' (1958) INSET: 'FIRST TRAVELLING SALESLADY' (1955)

be guaranteed, and receipts from advertising and sponsorship were forthcoming within a very short space of time. And if most of the shows were rubbish, still most people preferred watching rubbish in the comfort of their own homes to watching it down at the cinema.

Even more to the point, television was a new and dynamic industry. Here innovation could be nurtured in the womb of financial certainties. Soon television would be producing superior work in those genres that Hollywood producers assumed they owned the copyright to. Particularly westerns.

❝ I was never an extrovert, but I longed for independence even though I got along great with my parents . . . . Still I didn't know what I really wanted to do. I was never that fortunate to know ❞

As the television audience went up so the cinema audience went down. From a post-war maximum cinema attendance of some eighty-five to ninety million weekly, the figures dropped to a low of some thirty-five million weekly in 1956. Technical innovations like Stereo sound, Cinerama and 3-D — designed to offer spectacles with which television could not compete — failed to reverse the slide. Selling off film libraries in bulk to eager television companies provided a financial respite but little else. Some companies started thinking in terms of specific markets, others began the difficult process of converting to production specifically for television. All of them cut-back their costs.

TOMORROW THE BREAD LINE

One way of cutting costs was to make fewer films. Hollywood studios made less than two hundred films in 1959, compared to the four hundred produced in 1951. Another way was to dispense with the services of excess contract actors. In 1956, after eighteen months' work, Eastwood was dropped by Universal. "In those days they used to have a guy who looked like all their current guys, and I didn't look like anybody who was a current contract star, so they finally dumped me."

His film career during those eighteen months was hardly a success. He made fourteen appearances, but only six had any substance to them, if three or four lines merit such an accolade. In *Revenge Of The Creature* (the sequel to *The Creature From the Black Lagoon*) you had to be quick to spot him; in *Tarantula* you had to be psychic, since his one line was delivered from behind pilot's goggles. He was also credited on *Lady Godiva, Francis In the Navy, Star In The Dust* (his first western) and *Never Say Goodbye*. In the last-named he played, not for the first time, a lab assistant to Rock Hudson's macho professor. It was his most important part to date — he had four lines to say — and the director wanted him to wear glasses for it, to "give me a little more of an intellectual look, or a physician's assistant look, if there is such a thing." After searching at length for a suitable pair and finally getting used to the idea of wearing them, Hudson walked onto the set, took one look at Eastwood, and demanded a pair of his own. He got the glasses and Clint went without.

Though hardly a success at Universal, Eastwood now seems to have been bitten by the movie bug. He went straight to Howard Hughes' RKO-Radio Pictures, and made *The First Travelling Saleslady* and *Escapade In Japan* before Hughes shut down RKO in 1957. Eastwood went freelance, surviving on a little television work (including playing a cop in *Highway Patrol*) and some film walk-on parts, but mostly by digging swimming-pools for a contractor. In 1957 he appeared in a western — *Ambush At Cimarron Pass* ("the lousiest western ever made", he says, but also his biggest part to date) — and in William Wellman's World War One story *Lafayette Escadrille*. These appearances were hardly enough to survive on, but looking back from the vantage point of superstardom Eastwood considers his past difficulties with affection. "Made me go out and struggle" he says with a smile.

Meanwhile, television was taking great strides forward. *Wagon Train*, one of the pioneer one-hour series, was doing spectacularly well and Charles

> ‘I was a bit of a screw-up, a loner. Basically, I'm a drifter, a bum. As it turns out I'm lucky because I'm going to end up financially well-off for a drifter’

Marquis Warren, creator and producer of the half-hour *Gunsmoke*, sold CBS TV an idea for their one-hour western series. Eastwood's agent tried to get him the lead, "but they wanted a 35 year-old guy and I didn't photograph old at all." Then one day he was visiting a friend at CBS, story consultant Sonia Chernus, who told him that CBS and Warren had decided to write in a part for a second, younger lead in the projected series. She introduced Eastwood to a CBS executive, Robert Sparks, and a screen-test was arranged. Eastwood was accepted for the part, and shooting was underway when the company got cold feet and shelved the whole idea. Eastwood went back to the breadline for a few months. And then, out of the blue, he learned that CBS had reconsidered. The show was about to be launched as a mid-season replacement. *Rawhide*, and Eastwood, had arrived.

20

CHAPTER 2
THE ZEN ART OF THE BOUNTY HUNTER (1959-68)

AS ROWDY YATES IN TWO SCENES FROM 'RAWHIDE' WITH PAUL BRINEGAR (WISHBONE) AND FAR LEFT: WITH KIM HUNTER

LEARNING TO BE LACONIC

At 8 pm Standard Time on 9th January, 1959 American viewers saw Gil Favor lean forward in his saddle and shout, without apparently opening his mouth: "git'em up, move'em out". The screen filled with dust and cattle, and Frankie Laine's voice, then and once a week for the next seven and a half years, rolled out of nowhere — "rollin, rollin, rollin, keep them dogies rollin, rawhide . . ."

Rawhide was based by Warren on two clearly recognisable sources: authentic accounts of life on the trail drive (particularly George C. Duffield's 'Trail-drovers Diary') and Howard Hawks' very successful 1948 film *Red River*. It was to be a high-quality series, vague historical authenticity brought to life by a plethora of respectable guest-stars. The characters though were allotted strictly by a formula that owed everything to Hollywood and nothing to authenticity. The leading two were, as in *Red River*, the experienced older man (Eric Fleming's trail boss, Gil Favor) and his young, somewhat reluctant, disciple (Clint Eastwood's ramrod, Rowdy Yates). On the one side restraint and dependability, on the other the bravado of youth. It was the staple partnership that so many western *series* have worked through. The young one was supposed to grow into the older one as they passed through the fires of adversity together. They shared the action, the emotional interest, and usually the females that appeared. But not the humour. In *Rawhide* this was supplied by the cook Wishbone (Paul Brinegar) and his idiot assistant Mushy. The rest were specialised wooden figures like Sheb Wooley the scout ("the water holes are dry up ahead, Mr Favor") and the horse-handler Jesus (pronounced Hay-soos). They filled in the gaps. The guest stars supplied the week's plot and so set the whole process in motion. Meantime the cattle were prodded northwards towards the railhead at Sedalia, and the crew met up with all the natural hazards and moral dilemmas that Hollywood TV writers are prone to shuffle in their pursuit of a reasonable living.

True to the spirit of the times (the 1950s, not the 1870s) the nature of Western society was never really touched upon. The frontier was a door to open; civilisation the bride to be carried across the bloody threshold. That the frontier might be a door better left closed occurred to few; notions of civilisation as a double-edged sword to even less. The Indians were usually more of a natural hazard than a moral dilemma. Violence was nasty rather than endemic, and people shot through the head did not bleed profusely, which perhaps accounted for their never-failing ability to make moving dying speeches. You could tell which were the nasty men because they looked it, and because they always drew first but shot second if at all. From time to time each member of the team had a personal problem which proved soluble; all of them were tried for murder and acquitted at least once. Women came and reluctantly went. There was no sex. Drinking was allowed only in moderation, except at the end of the drive when everyone was expected to get drunk, spend all their wages, and sign on again. 'When you pass Sedalia you may collect $200'. *Rawhide* then was plot-wise not much better or worse than its many competitors: *Wagon Train, Bonanza, Cheyenne, Tenderfoot, Bronco* et al. If it was more enjoyable than most much of the credit belonged to Eric Fleming's laconic trail boss, a far more distinctive character than Eastwood's good-natured punk ramrod.

Clint though was far from unhappy. The boredom that afflicts many actors endlessly playing limited parts was alleviated by two things. One was memories of the dole queue and digging swimming-pools. The other was the opportunities it gave him to learn. He spent a great deal more time than most actors do with the technical crews, learning how a film is put together. The show generally had a different director each week, and these he

> ## Some people have a need to discuss deep, intimate things about themselves; discuss and analyse. I don't feel that need. Maybe it's a strength, maybe it's a weakness

observed at work, learning how to do certain things, and, sometimes, how not to do them. Acting-wise he began to experiment with his character. "One thing a series affords somebody," he says, "is a great security. In a series you know you are going to work every week. And if you try something one week and it doesn't work, you're going to be employed the next week; so it doesn't matter. So you can try anything you want and file all the things that work for you in your brain and discard what doesn't work. It's a great training ground." Most important of all, perhaps, he absorbed Eric Fleming's screen persona, that cool detachment which he would 'youthen' and amoralise in the 'Dollar' trilogy.

There were difficulties. He badly wanted to direct an episode, but CBS were not as keen on the idea. In one show he suggested that he take a camera, on horseback, into the middle of a stampede so as to get more exciting shots. He was told that it was against Union rules, which it wasn't. "I could see they didn't want to upset a nice standard way of movie-making." CBS did let him direct a few trailers for the show, but no more than that.

If this was frustrating the company's refusal to let him take part in chat shows or feature films during

his yearly lay-off was even more so. In the winter of 1961-2 he issued an ultimatum to his bosses via an interview with the *Hollywood Reporter*. "I've got open features in London and Rome that'll bring me more money in a year than the series has given me in three," he threatened. CBS didn't want to lose him, and he got what he wanted. The show was going well, still high in the ratings as it entered its fourth year.

But for some time no extra-curricular offers came Clint's way, and when one did it was from a strange source. Italy. One day his agent called to ask him if he liked the idea of a trip to Spain, to do a re-make of a Japanese film, funded by German, Spanish and Italian money, and directed by an unknown Italian, Sergio Leone. "Not particularly" he said.

'A PURPOSEFUL TENSION' (TURNING YEN INTO ZEN)

Leone's previous experience had mostly been in epics — Italian-style. The ingredients of this genre were massive spectacle, lots of laughs (occasionally

intentional), and, as often as not, the former Mr Universe, Steve Reeves. Outside Italy the atrocious dubbing gave many a European youth a good giggle. Leone had directed *Last Days Of Pompeii* and *Colossus Of Rhodes* in 1959-60, and co-directed *Sodom And Gomorrah* with the American director Robert Aldrich in 1962.

Leone was also an avid student of the history of the American West, and above all he wanted to make a western. 1963 was taken up in the search for the necessary financial backing. By the end of the year he had inveigled a triumvirate of production companies — Jolly Film (Rome), Constantin Film (Munich) and Ocean Film (Madrid) — into providing a budget of around $200,000. It wasn't a great deal, and the $25,000 demanded by Leone's first choice, James Coburn, was too much. Clint Eastwood, however, Leone was informed, would only cost $15,000. The director looked at *Rawhide*. "I didn't see any character . . . only a physical figure. What struck me most about Clint was his way of moving . . . it seemed to me Clint closely resembled a cat." The dynamic tension of Steve Reeves was about to give way to the dynamic lethargy of The

'Whatever success I've had is a lot of instinct and a little luck. I just go by how I feel'

Man With No Name.

The story-line was already waiting for him. Leone had bought the rights to Kurosawa's *Yojimbo*. In this film Toshiro Mifune plays a Samurai With No Name who arrives in a small community divided into two warring camps, sells himself first to one side and then the other, and between cracking jokes to himself decimates both. He leaves the corpse-strewn town muttering that "now we'll have a bit of peace around here". Notions of good and bad were conspicuous by their absence.

Leone's script moved the plot into the American West. Eastwood, still in California, looked at it. It was in English, but not very good English, since it had been written by Italians with little claim to bi-linguality. The western vernacular had obviously been dreamt up in Rome in front of a TV screen. But Eastwood liked it. "I felt maybe a European approach would give the western a new flavour, because I thought it had been in a very stagnant

31

period at that point." And the lead role was a far cry from the goody-goody Rowdy Yates. Here was a chance to broaden his repertoire, have a nice holiday in Europe, and pick up £15,000. It might have crossed his mind that Sturges' adaptation of Kurosawa's *The Seven Samurai* as *The Magnificent Seven* had been one of the most successful Westerns of recent memory, but it seems unlikely that he saw in this strange Italian script his own ticket to the superstar bracket.

Had Leone been as conventional a director as Sturges it most probably would not have been. But *A Fistful of Dollars* was clearly something out of the ordinary. The hero was no James Stewart or John Wayne figure who rode into town, gave the citizens an exam in higher morality, wiped out the failures, and ended up with the heroine. Most of the westerns being made around this time were as predictable as that.

As Clint observed of the traditional denouement: "two people are gonna get together and it isn't the guy and the horse". In *A Fistful of Dollars* the

> **People who go to movies like me. I never had any promotion or big studio build-up .... There are stars who are produced by the press — I am not one of them**

central character wins through, but his methods are neither predictable nor heroic in the traditional sense.

The film opens with a man riding slowly out of a desolate landscape and into a desolate town on a pretty desolate mule. He is wearing clothes normally associated with Mexican extras. The first sight that greets his eyes is a woman apparently being held prisoner and a child being kicked. He looks long and hard and . . . rides on. The main street is not packed with thriving humanity engaged in making the West a safe place to raise children in. It contains four sneering gunmen who shoot up the ground from under the mule's feet. The stranger careers inelegantly down the street, eventually jumping off outside the ubiquitous saloon.

None of this seems to disturb his sang-froid. It is only on discovering that the town is run by two warring gangs — one headed, naturally enough, by the sheriff — that he finds a reason for avenging the insult to his dignity. He wanders back up the street, kills all four gunmen, and then hires himself out to the opposing side on the strength of this virtuosity.

CLINT IN A PUBLICITY SHOT AFTER THE RELEASE OF 'A FISTFUL OF DOLLARS'

Although western 'heroes' do not normally have such a whole-hearted devotion to their own pockets, Eastwood's persona seems wholly in tune with its environment. His claim to heroism rests on no superior moral stand, no devotion to Love or the Law. Neither does it rest on an indifference to human life. Everyone is indifferent to that. It rests partly on his strength, determination and skill with a gun (the traditional values of the American western hero), but even more on his use of intelligence (the traditional European value) to manipulate his environment. For most of the film he happily plays one side off against the other, securing payment from both for his services. When the conflict seems threatened by a truce he manages to get it started again. When one side captures an important member of the opposition he immediately kidnaps someone from the other side to even things up. Only towards the end of the film does this refreshing pragmatism become somewhat compromised. Understandably the stranger starts to feel a personal involvement after he has been beaten half to death by the sadistic Ramon (Gian Maria Volonte). Less satisfying is the scene in which he releases Ramon's mistress from captivity, re-unites her with husband and child, and sends them into the wilderness. This 'angel of the Lord' role seems somewhat inappropriate. Such concessions to tradition were not to re-appear in *For A Few Dollars More*.

This brief sketch of the film's plot, in itself almost identical to *Yojimbo*, only touches the surface of the film's revolutionary appeal. In some ways — the incredible twists of the plot, the stranger's unbelievable skill with his gun — the Leone western is far less realistic than its traditional counterpart. But in

> ## When I first saw Yojimbo, I thought 'Geez, this would make a great western, only nobody would ever have the nerve to make it with this style'

themes. Staig and Williams in their *Italian Western; The Opera of Violence* describe them thus: "a musically surrealistic panorama of strange cries, savage guitar chords, jangling bells and the cracking of whips. Grunts, groans and Indian-like shrieks adorn the panorama. The form is totally unlike anything American. The music is as hostile as the action, the close affiliation enters the realm of Opera."

Individual characters have individual themes; The Man With No Name an ominously carefree whistling tune, Colonel Mortimer (in *For A Few Dollars More*) an ominously twanging jaw harp. Instruments become representational; they are woven together in themes as the characters are woven through the plot. None of this perhaps would be of more than peripheral interest if Morricone's music was not so good, and so contemporary, in its own right. It was a major factor in making Leone's films an authentic 'voice of the sixties'.

Neither was the appearance of The Man With No

others it rests on surer ground than conventional mythology. The humanscape — buildings, clothes, faces, motivations — seem closer to historical reality. The women do not look like they've just left their dressing-room. This is not an environment where family life flourishes with western props. Life looks a hard struggle, as it must have been. The law, as everywhere, is as strong as the civilisation it serves, and in this setting, where conflict is more the norm than collaboration, it is corrupt and/or impotent. The people are as indifferent to their neighbours' lives as the land is to their own. It's a dog-eat-dog world. And still the dogs look hungry.

In the Italian western this world is not presented only in visual terms. The musical soundtrack is of almost equal importance. In conventional westerns the soundtrack score was mostly wallpaper, only becoming distressingly audible when a wash of strings announced emotion or a rumble of something else signalled tension. The music vaguely underpinned the action. Ennio Morricone's themes for the Leone films are more of a social collage accompanying the individual-based narrative

Name an historical accident. Clint Eastwood was not the only man moving swiftly up the ladder to stardom with a mixture of electric music and 'cool'. Bob Dylan and many less-talented performers were pursuing similar success, if without No Name's reluctance to open his mouth. It was an image for the times. No Name was self-sufficient, not given to discussing personal philosophies, sexist in his indifference to women rather than in his treatment of them. His use of violence was as beautifully choreographed as that of the hoodlums in *A Clockwork Orange*. He didn't get into messy fist-fights; always it was the clean angles of the gundown. The emotional significance of killing was not a pleasure in death but in the style of its delivery. The physical distance offered by the gun mirrored the emotional distance felt from the other.

Eastwood was ideally equipped for this role. His way of moving — 'resembling a cat' — expressed the confidence and menace of 'cool'; his soft voice, used so infrequently, expressed the reluctance to indulge

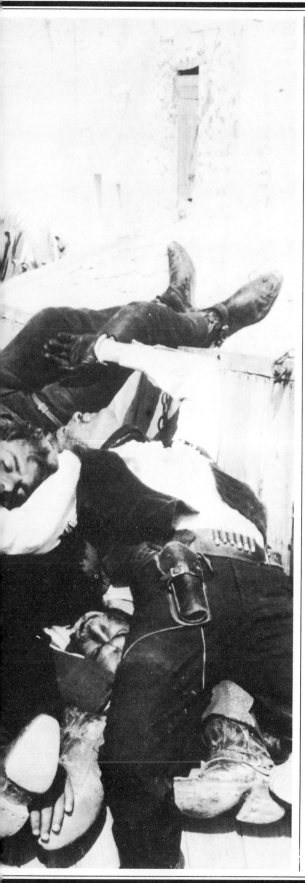

in meaningless communication. No Name was a man sufficient unto himself, as is the land. And like the land he was both beautiful and dangerous; strength clothed in rags, clear green eyes held in a perpetual squint, graceful hands hovering over a gun. The only obvious problem for Eastwood was the basic friendliness of his face, and in subsequent roles this has been hidden by cheroots, cigars, even, in *The Outlaw Josey Wales*, a disgusting habit of spewing out long streams of tobacco juice.

Eastwood's own contribution to his part seems to have been not inconsiderable, despite Leone's reluctance to give him any credit. He "made the part more anti-heroic . . . more of a guy who was a gun-man out for his own well-being, placed himself first, and didn't get involved in other people's problems unless it was to his benefit." As for mannerisms, it seems that it was Eastwood rather than Leone who turned The Man With No Name into the least talkative hero of western history. The script called for much more dialogue; Eastwood, with a knack for discarding dialogue that has remained one of his strongest traits, cut it to the bare minimum and beyond. The less No Name said the more mystery there remained locked away behind his eyes. The audience could draw their own conclusions as to what he felt, how he was motivated. In any case he was indisputedly in control.

FOR A FEW LIRE MORE

In Leone's films the land is important. In traditional westerns the land just lies around the towns; in Leone's the towns perch uneasily within the land. The land is usually empty. Desert valleys, bare mountains. By day the sun beats like a hammer on a dry anvil, by night the stars are as clear as ice. This is no place for softness, for relaxation. The Mongols came out of a land like this, to the eternal regret of their better-placed neighbours. *For a Few Dollars More* begins with a vast panorama of this emptiness. Through it, in the far distance, moves the tiny figure of a horseman, like a fly on a windowpane. Like the fly the horseman is too small for his environment. A rifle-shot cracks out and the figure crumples. 'Where life had no values', as the credits announce somewhat superfluously, 'death sometimes had its price'. The heroes of this film, we can safely assume, are unlikely to be social workers.

Enter Colonel Mortimer (Lee Van Cleef). As Morricone's heavenly choir and gunshots fade away we find him sitting on a train reading the Bible. Across the aisle sits an either half-dead or completely drunk Indian. The Colonel enquires as to when the train will reach Tucamcari and, on being informed that they will pass it in three or four minutes, proceeds to pull the communication cord. On being told by the conductor that such things are not allowed the Colonel reveals his gun. The conductor agrees that such things are allowed. At the Tucamcari ticket office the Colonel examines a wanted poster. The ticket-office man, palpably

'FOR A FEW DOLLARS MORE' (1965)

alone in the middle of nowhere, sniggers. It is difficult to imagine any other adequate response.

Cut to the Colonel entering a saloon. A man half-heartedly plays an out-of-tune piano, a dog wanders round, the barman looks bored out of his mind. The Colonel, with a little friendly persuasion, discovers that his quarry is upstairs. He goes up, slips the wanted poster under the door, stands aside as bullets rip from the inside, and then calmly wanders in past a woman screaming in a bath as his intended victim goes out of the window. The Colonel is in no hurry. He returns downstairs, walks out into the street — like the bar, empty — and with a flick of the wrist opens a professional kit attached to his saddle. Selecting a gun with the air of Jack Nicklaus choosing the right iron he shoots the horse from under his escaping victim and then, with infinite precision, fixes a longer hand-grip to his hand-gun, and turns it into a miniature rifle. With this he carefully kills his prey, who we now see for the first time. Like the Indian on the train, like the bar and street, his face is redolent with decay. Dirty, missing teeth, the look of a village idiot in his eyes. This is a real victim, no match at all for the professionalism of the hunter. Another fly on the window pane.

Another saloon, this time crowded. Enter Clint Eastwood, who still has no name, and who still wears the same poncho on his shoulders and cheroot in his mouth. He walks up to a card-game and takes over, dealing cards to one man and to himself. He wins. The man apprehensively asks what the stake had been. "Your life," says No Name. Ten seconds later the man and three cronies are dead all over the saloon and No Name is en route to the sheriff's office to collect his bounty. He doesn't criticise the sheriff for allowing wanted outlaws the run of his town; he merely removes the sheriff's badge — after collecting his money — and announces to no one in particular: "you people need a new sheriff".

So far nothing much, other than audience expectations built on a lifetime watching westerns, has been done to create any sympathy with those who appear to be successful. In a traditional Western this is the moment to introduce the hero, the one who is both successful and concerned with the higher moral order. The one who knows that the meek are blessed, not merely flies on a windowpane. But this is not that sort of world, and hence not that sort of western. A real old-style white-hatted hero would make Lee and No Name's hats look black. Leone, by introducing a blacker-than-black hatted villain instead makes Lee and No Name's hats look almost white. It's OK to treat people like flies when those who lead them act like scorpions.

Enter Indio, played by Gian Maria Volonte. The first we see of him he is butchering a family who have been accessories to his captivity. Unlike the Colonel and No Name he kills with relish, particularly the man, who he executes in a ritualised gunfight set to the tune of a musical watch. But this piece of theatre does not exorcise his rage and calm him down. Psychosis is his normal state. The drugs he uses don't stop him shaking, don't silence the noises in his head. He is clearly not a man the community can afford to take lightly, especially as he is planning to rob the supposedly impregnable El Paso bank.

Compared to this madman both No Name and the Colonel seem like civilisation's gift to the wilderness. They are already in El Paso, patiently waiting for Indio to stick his neck out far enough for a rich bounty to be claimed. It gradually dawns on them both that the other is there for the same reason and, after a playful confrontation has created a certain mutual respect, they form a partnership. "One on the inside, one on the outside" the Colonel decides professionally, and the reluctant No Name agrees to be the former. Here the division of character is drawn between the two: the Colonel's cool appraisal versus No Name's youthful bravado. No Name accepts the appraisal but can't resist asking the Colonel if he was "ever young?" The Colonel, fingering a musical watch similar to Indio's, says yes, and we are taken in a flashback to the rape and suicide of a girl who we later find out was the Colonel's sister. Indio was the culprit. This tells us a great deal about both the Colonel's motives and Indio's psychosis, but significantly nothing about No Name. His mystery remains intact.

From here on the film moves relentlessly on towards the climactic gunfight between Indio and the Colonel. The latter kills the former and generously gives No Name his share of the bounty. His and Indio's problems have been resolved in the only possible way. Only The Man With No Name, loading bodies into a cart and cheerfully counting dollars, goes out of the film the same way he came in. Save for a few dollars more.

'FOR A FEW DOLLARS MORE' (1965). RIGHT: LEE VAN CLEEF AS COLONEL MORTIMER

For A Few Dollars More introduces a number of Leone's favourite motifs, most notably the encapsulation of the past in musical instruments and the railroad as advance agent of capitalism's destruction of the old West. Both figure again, particularly in *Once Upon A Time In The West*. It was also important for Eastwood's persona. For one thing the presence of two other central characters enabled his to be better drawn, for another he was obviously allowing himself a slightly wider range of expression.

There is one scene in the film in which No Name is breaking one of Indio's friends out of jail as a passport for his own entry into the gang. No Name climbs up to the cell window and, watched by the dazed inmate, fixes sticks of dynamite to the bars. He then lights the fuse with his cheroot, flashes a beaming smile at the prisoner, and disappears out of sight. Seconds later the wall is blown apart.

There is a whole world-view behind that smile. It is the smile Newman and McQueen have perfected, a smile of awareness and the self-control it brings. Because there is nothing to lose; because audacity is cool. It is the smile that makes you a hero because it sets you above both the common herd and the authorities, the physical morass of the one, the moral morass of the other. It is the image that Eastwood, in garbs other than No Name's poncho, will make his own in the 1970s.

THE BAD, THE NOT-SO-BAD AND THE DOWNRIGHT VICIOUS

Some months before Leone started filming *For A Few Dollars More* in Spain, *A Fistful of Dollars* had been released in Italy to great popular acclaim. El Cigarillo, as No Name was immediately christened, became a cult figure; the film itself outgrossed both *Mary Poppins* and *My Fair Lady*, no mean feat for a mean film, earning itself some $7 million in the process.

Not only was the public infatuated. The Italian director Vittorio de Sica called Clint the "new Gary Cooper" and Sophia Loren, arriving in America, was astonished to hear that Americans only knew of him as a gangling cowboy in one of their myriad TV series. De Sica went further than compliments. He decided to direct Eastwood in his part of one of those Italian films built like a chain of large cameos. The film, *Le Streghe (The Witches)*, was designed as a showcase for the talents of the producer's wife, Silvana Mangano. She appeared in all five parts, East-

wood, as her husband, appeared in the fifth part, directed by De Sica, 'A Night Like Any Other'. He wore modern dress and glasses, which must at least have been a change. But the film hardly caught fire at the box office, nor enhanced his or De Sica's reputation. Variety called 'A Night Like Any Other' the "dismal, pointless De Sica bit at the end".

While the critics were churning out words Eastwood was churning out more *Rawhides*. He was now the trail boss since CBS, in a last dismal attempt to reverse the show's falling ratings, had sacked the peerless Eric Fleming. It was like amputating the head to save the body; it didn't work. Early in 1966 the series was terminated with seventeen scheduled episodes uncompleted. Eastwood got $119,000 compensation, had a rest, and set off once more for Spain.

Leone's bank balance was also looking much healthier as receipts started to come in for the first two films. The budget for *For A Few Dollars More* had been $600,000, Eastwood's share $50,000 plus a percentage. For the next film, *The Good, The Bad and The Ugly*, the budget was to be $1,200,000, of which $250,000 would go to Eastwood. He was on his way to becoming a millionaire.

No Name was also still engaged in the pursuit of wealth. The character doesn't change very much from film to film, but like the missing piece in a jigsaw his shape and colour becomes more apparent as the others are fitted into place. In *A Fistful Of Dollars* he was introduced, in *For A Few Dollars More* he was defined negatively in relation to his 'partner' and his adversary Indio, both themselves well-drawn characters. In *The Good, The Bad And The Ugly* he is placed squarely in a particular social situation, the American Civil War.

At first sight though, similarities between the films are more obvious than the differences. *The Good, The Bad And The Ugly*, opens, like the previous film, with the introduction, one by one, of the three central characters. Leone's love for upsetting western conventions is well illustrated by the first scene, in which two men arrive at one end of an empty town and one at the other. They stride purposefully down the street towards each other. Just when you expect the normal confrontation they all duck sideways into a building, gunshots are heard, and out of a window leaps Tuco (Eli Wallach) grasping a gun in one hand and a chicken leg in the other. The words 'Il Brutto' (The Ugly) flash across the screen.

Next, 'The Bad'. Setenza (Lee Van Cleef), otherwise known as Angel Eyes, arrives at an adobe dwelling to visit the owner-occupier. He lounges indolently in the doorway; he is not the sort of man who jumps through windows with chicken-legs in his hand. He doesn't talk much either, merely radiating a sadistic pleasure in the other's obvious terror. They sit down to eat, and Angel Eyes extracts the information he has been hired to extract. In the process he hears of an Army cashbox that has been stolen and hidden; this will provide the film's continuity. In the meantime his unfortunate confidante, realising that Angel Eyes has been hired to kill him as well, makes a generous counter-offer for Angel

GBU 4

Eyes' services in killing the man who originally hired him. This Angel Eyes takes, but then ruefully admits that he always carries through his contracts and dispatches the man and his elder son with obvious relish. He returns to his original employer with the same message, pulling the pillow over his head and pouring about five bullets through it. This is fulfilling contractual obligations with a vengeance. 'The Bad' comes as something of an understatement.

These two characters, Tuco and Angel Eyes, are an interesting inversion of Indio and Colonel Mortimer. Now the professional is the psychotic, and the noisy, garrulous Mexican the more endearing character. Not that Tuco is any less vicious than Angel Eyes, but his primitive and animalistic violence is much more acceptable than Angel Eyes' cold-blooded professional sadism. And it is Tuco

Italian actors come from the Hellzapoppin' school of drama. To get my effect I stayed impassive and I guess they thought I wasn't acting. All except Leone who knew what I was doing

who will partner No Name this time. Not Cool and Cool versus Garrulous Psychotic, as in *For A Few Dollars More*, but Cool and Garrulous versus Psychotic Cool.

No Name makes his appearance in time to kill three men who have just captured Tuco for his bounty. Tuco is overjoyed until he realises that No Name wants the bounty as well. And not only once. No Name has a plan. As Tuco is about to be hanged No Name shoots away the rope and rescues him. They share the money and call in on another community with the same scheme. Again Tuco is delivered up to justice and whisked away as it is about to be executed. The whole scheme has a kind of mad humour behind it. Neither Tuco nor Angel Eyes would ever have conceived it. The one lacks the logic, the other the imagination. Only No Name has both. This is what makes him all-aware, what makes him smile. And this in the end will make him successful.

Meanwhile Angel Eyes is working his way down the chain that leads to the hidden cashbox, looking for a man named Bill Carson. No Name and Tuco, with rather less single-mindedness, are playfully trying to dispose of each other. No Name abandons Tuco in the middle of a desert, seventy miles from

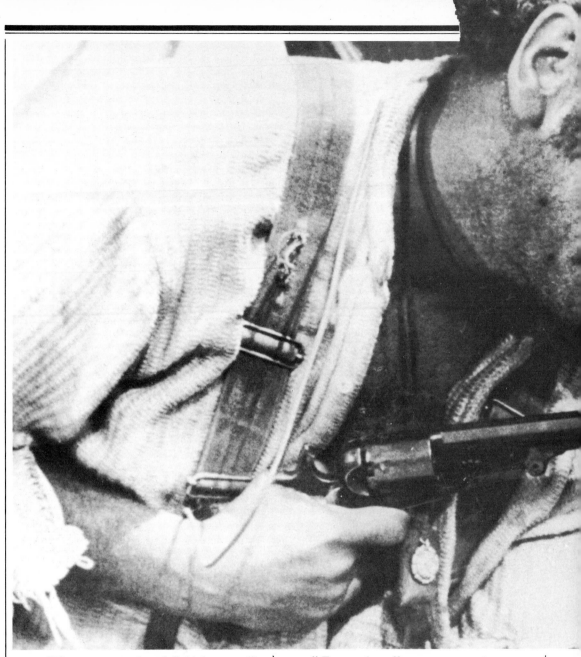

water. "If you save your breath I think a man like you could manage it", he says respectfully. Tuco does manage it, and comes after No Name. Catching him in a hotel he is just about to hang him when a shell from the increasingly-evident Civil War crashes through the roof and sends Tuco through the floor. Unperturbed by this setback he follows the trail of No Name's cheroot butts across country and re-captures him. He then drags him across the desert, watching him suffering with a vindictive glee from under a fetching pink parasol. Eventually tiring of this sport he is about to finish off the half-dead No Name when a driverless carriage swoops past full of dead and dying Confederate soliders. One of them is Bill Carson. "$200,000" he croaks as Tuco is about to put an end to his misery. Tuco's face lights up. "Where?" he asks. "In Sad Hill Cemetery". "Which grave?" "First bring me

water." Tuco rushes off to get water, and returns to find No Name lying next to a dead Bill Carson. No Name has the name of the grave, Tuco the name of the cemetery. Now they need each other. Tuco, suddenly full of concern for No Name's lamentable condition, takes him to a nearby mission run by his priest-brother.

Leone's presentation of the American Civil War is crucial to the definition of his characters, and it is important to remember in this respect that Leone himself spent his adolescent years amidst the horrors of modern war. The American Civil War and the Second World War were, in some states and countries respectively, 'popular' conflicts. In the East and in northern Europe conflicting ideals were seen as a reason for fighting, possible tickets to glory. But in the American West and Italy this was far less true. Here the suffering, the indiscriminate maiming and

killing, were not alleviated by such a sense of purpose. Here the war was imposed on mostly unwilling participants. It brought ruin, and receded leaving only the nihilism born of futility. The only response that made sense to many was that adopted by No Name and Tuco. Ignore the war as much as possible, and try to make use of it when it can't be ignored, rather like laissez faire businessmen confronting the Inland Revenue. Against the purposelessness of social slaughter for invisible ideals they pose purposeful personal slaughter for solid gold. The grim reality of civilisation meets the grim reality of the frontier.

The face of war depicted by Leone rings miserably true. The coachload of dead soldiers, the mission full of wounded, the Confederate spy crucified on a railroad engine's cowcatcher. When a soldier is shot in the street of a half ruined town there is no *Paths Of Glory* melodrama.

It is all over in about twenty seconds; the soldiers marching by do not even bother to watch. Even those still alive are ghosts, a point brilliantly observed in the Yankee column covered from head to toe in grey dust. Eventually No Name and Tuco blunder into a fully-fledged battle, with Yankee and Confederate armies deployed on either side of a riverbridge that both wish to capture. The Yankee captain, who has to stay drunk to function at all, dreams of blowing up the bridge,

47

1 No Name and Tuco start up the street. At the far end Angel Eyes' three gunmen cross over and begin to move down behind the buildings on the north side.

2 One of the gunmen goes through a building to a window but is seen and killed by Tuco. The others are working their way around to our heroes' rear.

4 The smoke clears and the two are shot down by No Name and have used the diversion to gain advantageous positions.

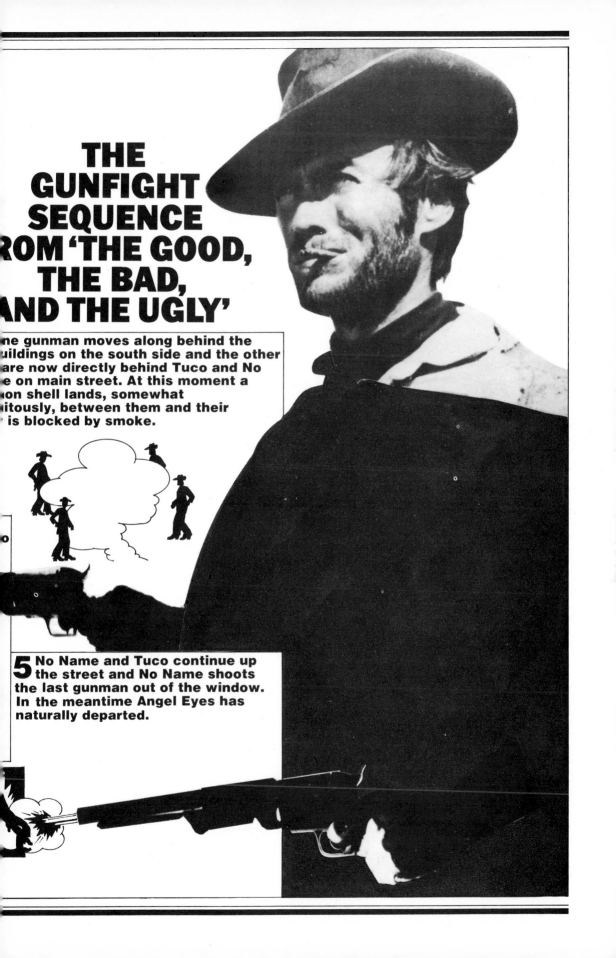

THE GUNFIGHT SEQUENCE FROM 'THE GOOD, THE BAD, AND THE UGLY'

ne gunman moves along behind the
uildings on the south side and the other
are now directly behind Tuco and No
e on main street. At this moment a
on shell lands, somewhat
itously, between them and their
is blocked by smoke.

5 No Name and Tuco continue up
the street and No Name shoots
the last gunman out of the window.
In the meantime Angel Eyes has
naturally departed.

50

but unfortunately has orders to take it intact regardless of the cost. No Name and Tuco have no such inhibitions, particularly as Sad Hill Cemetery is on the other side of a river that they can't cross whilst two armies are straddling it. Blow up the bridge, as No Name observes philosophically, and they'll go and fight somewhere else. This they do. The captain dies happy and the armies are gone the next morning.

Having recognised the tragic farce of social authority the film returns to basics for the final gundown. Angel Eyes arrives on cue and the classic three-cornered contest is held amidst Sad Hill's circle of death. In such a world, and in such a contest, it is advisable to have an 'edge'. No Name, unbeknownst to the other two, has already unloaded Tuco's gun. Angel Eyes, his attention divided by not knowing this, is outgunned; Tuco is left rich but horseless. No Name rides away over the hill and into legend.

CHE GUEVARA AND OTHER TRADITIONAL WESTERNS (OR THE MARXIST-LEONEIST HERO)

The stranger who arrives unheralded, turns a situation upside-down, and finally rides back alone into the wilderness is a staple character of the Western genre. Unlike The Man With No Name he usually has one — *Shane* is the classic example — but rarely a defined past or a settled future. He has no ties. He can have none, for learning the art of survival in the alien land of the West has taken him beyond the trammels of civilisation that the majority still live within. In a sense he has gone 'native', become a white Indian. He flows with the forces of nature and with the violent insecurity of frontier life. To him they are often one and the same. He accepts the West as it is; he has none of the neuroses that civilisations breed. And so he is in control of his environment, much as the surfer is in control of the wave.

The Eastwood persona is in many ways an updating of this traditional figure. He too has the attributes of the romantic hero: solitariness, self-sufficiency, a mastery of his environment and of himself. It is most evident not in the trappings of power but in his state of mind, particularly his sense of humour. When the Man With No Name smiles it is always with a vaguely condescending amusement. It is the smile of awareness confronting the lack of it in others. It is never the sadistic glee born of fear that characterises everyone else (Colonel Mortimer excepted) in the Dollar trilogy.

These are the traditional attributes, but the character created by Leone and Eastwood goes further. Shane and his successors carried a vivid double message; on the one hand inviting hero worship for their mastery, on the other inviting satisfaction that this mastery was being wielded for the benefit of its antithesis: the civilising of the West. It is not Shane who wins but the farmer whom he helps. Civilisation is left to prosper while Shane himself rides away into a lonely immortality, the doomed hero of a passing age. In most traditional westerns the hero is the means, not the end. Either he rides off with his heroism, leaving the community safer for his visit, or he himself is seduced by the community. He becomes a lawman, buys a ranch, falls in love, sometimes all three. He settles. He stops moving. He is brought back within the trammels and so loses the control that life outside them made possible. At this point the film has to end because the hero is no longer heroic.

In the Leone films none of this occurs. The communities that are portrayed are not flourishing towns well on the way to embourgeoisment. They are decaying, decadent, left behind by the random

> **There are two kinds of actors. One sits in the dressing room waiting for his call, and the other gets out into the business and polishes his craft by absorbing everything**

march of progress or half-destroyed by the random virus of war. The Man With No Name encounters none of those women who traditionally appear in time to save the hero from his heroism. Even more striking, he never gets involved in fist-fights. No one, male or female, ever touches him physically, ever begins to tear at the shell which his exile from civilisation has required him to create. He remains a virginal figure in a virgin land, invulnerable, free from neuroses. He searches for money, but to no apparent purpose. There is no double message. The virtues of the frontier are exalted; there is no corresponding pull from the side of civilisation.

It is not too hard to see why these films were made in the sixties, or why they proved so popular. It was a decade of revolt, sandwiched between the false optimism of the fifties and the unalleviated pessimism of the seventies. There were many reasons for this revolt, but one connecting thread was clearly a growing feeling that people were slowly losing control over their own lives. And there were many ways in which it was expressed, two of them were indisputably the cult of indifference, of stylish 'cool', and the use of revolutionary violence. For such a social situation it is hard to imagine a more fitting hero

than The Man With No Name, who is in control of his life and environment, who smiles knowingly and bows to no one, who looks good and keeps free of ties, who kills with a passionless artistry. The image was a little like Che Guevara's, except that Guevara was tied to a dream of the future, to a higher morality and an economic theory. No Name is Guevara without the encumbrances, without a future, a permanent revolution that will never risk the corrupton of statehood.

NO NAME STARTS COLLECTING BADGES

Lenin once said something to the effect that, at crucial moments, the workers had more idea of what was going on than the Party. The same could be said of the cinema public and cinema critics. When, in early 1967, *A Fistful of Dollars* at last reached the American screen the critics were less than effusive in their welcome. "High blown cowboy camp" one magazine said. The film was accused of "violating the happy romantic myth" of the West, one criticism which Leone must have enjoyed. Cue Magazine described *For A Few Dollars More*, released later the same year, as "a big nothing . . . the acting is a bore, the plot second-rate". Many agreed that the films were too long and, above all, too violent.

The much-respected critic Paulene Kael found the films to be entertainingly larger-than-life. It is only since the release of Eastwood's controversial '*Dirty Harry*' trilogy that she has re-reviewed them to find the early signs of what she finds so offensive in the later films. Indeed, one could do no better than quote from her original review of Kurosawa's *Yojimbo* for an understanding of the innovatory power of Leone's films: "Of all art forms, movies are most in need of having their concepts of heroism undermined . . . the western has always been a rather hypocritical form. The hero represents a way of life that is becoming antiquated. The solitary defender of justice is the last of the line; the era of lawlessness is over, the courts are coming in. But the climax is the demonstration that the old way is the only way that works — though we are told that it is the last triumph of violence . . . *Yojimbo* employs an extraordinary number of the conventions of the form, but takes hypocrisy for a ride . . . " Anticipating criticism of the movie's amoral violence she adds: "movies are, happily, a popular medium, but does that mean that people must look to them for confirmation of their soggiest humanitarian sentiments."

Like Kurosawa, Leone took hypocrisy for a ride. And that ride took Clint Eastwood into the superstar bracket. The public loved the 'Dollar' films, flocking in the proverbial droves to see The Man With No Name wander across their desert. The smell of money naturally reached the well-attuned noses of Hollywood, and offers started coming in to Eastwood from the industry which had discarded him a decade before. United Artists, to whom Eastwood

had contractual obligations wanted a western; Eastwood Out West seemed a box-office certainty. They offered him $400,000 and 25% of the net take, something of an improvement on the $75 a week of Universal extra days.

Clint at this time must have been taking his first long holiday in many a year. He had returned from filming *The Good, The Bad And The Ugly* in the Autumn of 1966, and for the first time did not have to leap back into the role of Rowdy Yates. It must have seemed a good idea, career-wise, to make another western. He might have returned in triumph, but he still had to establish himself as more than Leone's man in a poncho. This was no time to take risks.

But however reasonable the decision it was artistically rather unfortunate. Comparisons with the Leone films were bound to be made, and in that harsh light *Hang 'Em High* is not a very good film. Leone, like few directors before him — Ford and Mann are the only parallels — had transformed the western. He had given it a new intensity, both in the depth of theme and in the surface style. These two facets had been inseparably welded to make a convincing whole. In *Hang 'Em High* there was only the new style; the content was strictly traditional.

Ted Post, chosen (presumably by Eastwood) to direct, had worked on several *Rawhide* episodes. He got on well with Clint, and has since been named by him as one of the three directors who most influenced him, the others being Leone and Don Siegel. It seems unlikely that Eastwood learnt anything about depth of theme from Post. Technically there was nothing to complain about in *Hang 'Em High;* it is what is absent rather than what is present that is conspicuous. Leone's westerns are more than westerns. *Hang 'Em High*, despite its contemporary styling, is not.

All has not been lost. The attention to historical accuracy, which characterises Leone's backcloths if not his central characters, is still commendable. Fort Grant in the film is a reasonable depiction of Fort Smith, Judge Fenton a fair portrait of the famous hanging-Judge Parker whose stomping-ground it was. The public hangings with their bizarre mixture of commercialism and bible singing, the brothel with its sternly upright madame — both convey the uneasy blending of crude frontier violence with the repressed authoritarianism of civilisation which were typical of the times. The heroine too is refreshingly real. Through this social uncertainty Eastwood's Deputy-Marshal Jed Cooper moves with most of the assurance, if none of the mystery, of The Man With No Name. Most significant, he has no sense of humour. Eastwood gives the sort of performance that is expected: strong, mostly silent, single-minded in his determination to avenge his near-lynching with which the film begins. But he is never in control of the situation as The Man With No Name was. In fact he is almost controlled by it. Sometimes he is even confused.

He is not the only one. The themes supposedly underlying his pursuit of the vendetta remain annoyingly vague. It is obvious that someone is trying to

say something about the different kinds of justice — legal, vigilante, private — but exactly what is hard to fathom. The thrust of the plot seems to suggest that only through the Law can justice be long-term effective, yet the audience is left with the efficacy of Cooper as dispenser of his own justice and the seeming hypocrisy of legal justice as presented in the public execution sequences. Civilisation wins all right — Jed keeps his badge — but the rough and ready justice of the individual remains both morally

acceptable and more watchable. This distinction will become more problematic as Eastwood moves into modern dress for *Coogan's Bluff* and the 'Dirty Harry' trilogy.

It may or may not have occurred to Eastwood that *Hang 'Em High* was a somewhat unsatisfactory film. The fact that several years were to pass before he returned West (other than for the musical *Paint Your Wagon*) suggests that it did. It seems likely that the making of the film — his relationship with Ted Post must have been much more a relationship of equals than the accepted norm of director-actor relationships — taught him how much more there was to learn. He needed to work with other directors and broaden his repertoire of roles. Working with Leone had taught him a great deal — *Hang 'Em High* demonstrated both how much and how little — but he was now in need of a powerful American influence. And as it turned out Don Siegel needed him too.

55

CHAPTER 3
THE RED BADGE OF RECTITUDE (1968-71)

EASTWOOD HO!

The film opens with an image of cliched familiarity — the rolling sands and rocky crags of the mythic West. A savage Indian camps out in the hills. Oh yes, this is a Clint Eastwood film Bluff? That's some kind of cliff, isn't it? A piece of geology like the ones that litter John Ford's Monument Valley.

To those brought up on westerns — and they very definitely include Clint Eastwood fans — the associations are obvious and immediate. No sooner has *Coogan's Bluff* begun than you expect to see The Man With No Name riding in over the horizon. But *Coogan's Bluff* marks a transition for the Eastwood character and the opening sequence is a cleverly executed *trompe l'oeuil*. When No Name does make his appearance he rides into the old West in a jeep. The Indian picks up a high-powered rifle with a telescopic sight. This is the twentieth century.

Coogan's Bluff is the first American Eastwood picture to look like a picture of America. *Hang 'Em High*, although made in America with American money, still looks like a 'spaghetti western'. It does prefigure later developments in the Eastwood character, by giving him a name, a badge of office and a sex life — all of which become staples of the character in later films. But *Hang 'Em High* was made by United Artists in 1967 essentially to cash in on the reputation of the 'spaghetti westerns' — only just being released in America — and Eastwood wears his name, badge and sex with as much studied casualness as No Name wore his poncho. *Coogan's Bluff*, on the other hand, takes Eastwood right out of the mythic West and into historical America.

Of course, *Coogan's Bluff* is a western — and Eastwood's Deputy Sheriff Walt Coogan is a western hero. But director Don Siegel has played one of his favourite tricks with this movie. By setting most of the action in New York City he has taken an established genre of Hollywood movies and given it the depth of a realistic social setting. Eastwood as Coogan plays out his gunfighter's role against the backdrop of twentieth century life — in the streets of *the* twentieth century city, New York. He becomes the focus for a number of dramatic conflicts — between the old West and the East Coast image of the USA; between frontier morality and the civilised code; between the romanticised individual and the mundane collectivity of bureaucracy; between, in the last analysis, the social myth that used to be called 'the American Dream' and the social reality of coercion and compromise.

These are conflicts that Eastwood carries into most of his subsequent films. For Eastwood "the basis of drama is conflict", but in the 'spaghetti westerns' it was simply conflict between characters, manifested in the shoot-out. And yet even the shoot-outs had a level at which deeper conflict registered. The popularity of No Name seems to have stemmed from his image as a still, certain point in a chaotic world. It's to Eastwood's credit that he removed a lot of the dialogue from *A Fistful Of Dollars*, thus establishing a persona appropriate to a sixties' superman. "My point-of-view," says East-

wood, "was the more the leading character talked the less mystique he had, the more dissipated the strength of the film." Indeed, No Name's muteness did not suggest stupidity, as one might have expected. On the contrary, it suggested power and certainty. Action (and Eastwood firmly believes in action films) became the knife edge cutting through the doubts and confusions which, while absent from the films themselves, were seen by the young audience as their inheritance from a dying world. No Name kept quiet on screen and so became an appropriate symbol of all those who might have been taking to the streets of San Francisco, Chicago, Paris, London or Prague.

It was an image that reverberated down the ages. It was worn by the mythic gallant knights of old and by their latter-day descendants — hard-boiled private eyes like Philip Marlowe and Sam Spade, the Gregory Peck character in Henry King's *The Gunfighter*, almost every character ever played by Humphrey Bogart, even real people like Che Guevara and

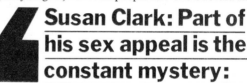

Susan Clark: Part of his sex appeal is the constant mystery: how deeply does he feel; how deeply is he involved with life?

Bob Dylan. People who did things and didn't have to talk about it. It echoed two of the great, posthumous, gurus of the sixties — Lao Tze, the zen master, when he wrote "Those who say do not know, those who know do not say", and Karl Marx, the revolutionary, when he wrote "Philosophers have only interpreted the world; the point, however, is to change it."

Walt Coogan is different. He is from contemporary Arizona. After capturing the Indian at the start of the film, Coogan visits a girl on the way back to town. He ties the Indian to a railing, as an old-time cowboy might have done with a horse. The sheriff interrupts Coogan to tell him that he must go to New York to extradite a prisoner, Ringerman (Don Stroud), and bring him back for trial.

Coogan arrives in New York in cowboy hat and boots. Ringerman is in hospital recovering from a bad drug trip and the city police, in the shape of Lt. McElroy (Lee J. Cobb), tell Coogan that Ringerman can't be released into his custody. At the police station, Coogan meets a social worker, Julie (Susan Clark), and although he is attracted to her they argue when Coogan hits one of her clients whom she has been allowing to fondle her. Coogan decides to get his prisoner out of hospital and return to Arizona.

Bluffing his way into the hospital he finds Ringerman with his girlfriend, Linny Raven (Trisha Sterling). He tells Ringerman to get dressed, thus

echoing the opening words of the film when he tells the Indian "Okay, chief. Put your pants back on." Ringerman and Coogan go to the heliport where Coogan is beaten up by three men acting under Raven's instructions. Ringerman escapes.

Visited in his hospital ward by Lt. McElroy, Coogan is told to lay off the case. He refuses and discharges himself from hospital. He tracks Raven down to a crowded discotheque and makes love to her. Thinking she has told him Ringerman's hideout he arrives at a pool-hall where he is beaten up by six men — again acting on Raven's instructions. He returns to her apartment where he threatens to kill her. She leads him to Ringerman's real hideout in Fort Tryon Park and after a motorcycle chase, Coogan finally captures Ringerman.

After going through the proper procedure, Coogan and his prisoner fly back to Arizona. Waving goodbye at the heliport is Julie wearing a red dress — the colour associated with the violence surrounding Coogan. Inside the helicopter, Coogan gives Ringerman a cigarette — something he refused to do when the Indian asked for one at the beginning of the film.

Even this brief sketch shows that *Coogan's Bluff* is thematically a far more complex film than the 'spaghetti westerns' and that Walt Coogan is far from the virtually monomaniacal No Name. No Name is essentially a hunter, his heroic stature stems from his isolation and the ultimate virtue of his actions is determined by his power and skill. This is Coogan as he first appears — the cool, distant hero surviving the encroachment of civilisation in a pocket of the old West. He is not amoral, unlike his predecessor. Virtue is his to some extent by reason of his prowess, his ability to dominate in person-to-person conflict. But this prowess — the power that comes out of the barrel of his gun — is put in the service of the law. And the law is a set of rules, according to Coogan and his ilk, designed to codify a higher morality, "the public good".

In the middle of the Mojave desert, Coogan is able to preserve his independence and to enforce the law according to his own code. His flight to New York is a flight into mass society, where personal codes are no longer workable and where problems arise precisely because the enforcement of the law is itself subject to a public code.

The complexities arising out of Coogan's arrival in the big city are revealed through a series of associations. Ringerman is identified with the Indian, especially from Coogan's point-of-view (they are both savages — hardly better than the hunter's quarry). The final motorcycle chase echoes the horse chase of a traditional western. Julie and Coogan are, at first, natural antagonists — although their enmity is due only to a differing interpretation of the legal rules. As a social worker she represents the liberal establishment, while Coogan stands for the conservative individualist. By the end of the film Julie and Coogan have found some common ground. In the same way, Coogan becomes closer to Ringerman. His search for Ringerman means that he has to assume some of Ringerman's characteristics (as any

When in Southern California visit Universal Studios

THE MAN WITH NO NAME TAKE
ON A KILLER WITH NO FEAR O
A MAN-HUNT WITH NO RULES

UNIVERSAL Presents

CLINT EASTWOOD
in COOGAN'S BLUFF

CO-STARRING

SUSAN CLARK · DON STROUD · TISHA STERLING · BETTY FIELD

LEE J. COBB

SCREENPLAY BY
HERMAN MILLER, DEAN RIESNER and HOWARD RODMAN

STORY BY
HERMAN MILLER

PRODUCED AND
DIRECTED BY
DON SIEGEL

EXECUTIVE
PRODUCER
RICHARD E. LYONS

IN COLOR · A UNIVERSAL PICTURE

 Suggested For Mature Audiences

good hunter would do with his or her prey). Coogan visits the places Ringerman hangs out in; he meets his mother; sleeps with his girlfriend. To some extent he adopts Ringerman's identity — even occupying Ringerman's place in hospital.

All this serves to build a picture of Coogan as a complex character — a citizen of the United States in the late sixties. That his name is constantly confused by city officialdom (McElroy calls him "Tex" or "Wyatt", rejecting his real western origins in favour of mythic ones) only makes Coogan's character more credible. The monomaniacs in *Coogan's Bluff* are the bureaucrats, incapable of stretching a point of procedure, seeing only means and not ends and with imaginations that reach no further than the city limits. Even Ringerman has his subtleties, because he (and Coogan, for that matter) is brutalised by the city in the same way that the Indian is brutalised by reservation life. Reservations and cities — in a word civilisation — are the enemies. As Coogan himself says, gazing on a rooftop view of Manhattan, "I'm just trying to picture how it was before people fouled it up".

PROPHETS WITHOUT HONOUR

Asked if he was really like the cop he so often plays, Eastwood once replied: "Certain things that come out of the collage of characters you play *are* you; certain elements of the person can't be withheld. I suppose I feel that way, I suppose that's why I play it well. Other people can't play that. Open people, more extroverted people maybe, can't play that kind of character, because they don't feel that way. They don't feel alone and they're lonely alone, if you know what I mean — they're not happy alone. They act real well in circumstances where, maybe, there are a lot of people and relationships going in. I guess that's somewhat because of the way I am."

On the other hand, as he is often at pains to point out, Clint Eastwood is an actor, not a cowboy or a cop, and he doesn't necessarily reproduce himself on screen. But it is precisely his approach to acting that allows a parallel to be made between Eastwood the man and Eastwood the character. The Method school of acting which begat Brando, Dean and Newman in the fifties is not to Eastwood's taste. On several occasions in the fifties it stood between him and a part, and the very modishness of Method acting clearly turned him against it. Eastwood is not an actor who believes in becoming or even empathising with his character. On the contrary, he believes that the limitations of his repertoire are essential to his talent. "I hardly think of myself as playing Hamlet," he says, "or Oedipus or somebody from Noel Coward. Any of them [his later roles] may be said to be different from my country bandit image, but playing them has not been a matter of trying to become a different kind of actor. I played them because they were roles that interested me, that I knew I could handle."

And while Eastwood is not a violent man, the

violence of his characters bears the seal of approval of his own beliefs about society. Dramatic violence, for Eastwood, must emerge naturally from the conflicts and tensions which form the drama. He is a very important factor in the final shape of his films — he is not only a director in his own right; he is not only among the select band of actors who can determine their own price. He is a surprisingly articulate and intelligent man who has consistently contributed ideas and assistance as well as image to the films he appears in. It was Eastwood who approved Siegel for *Coogan's Bluff*, and Eastwood directed parts of *Dirty Harry* when Siegel was ill. The establishment of his own production company at the end of the sixties (Malpaso), only formalised what had long been an informal concern with the whole process involved in the creation of his films.

This aspect of his career gives weight to Eastwood's principled approval of his cinematic image. "I like those characters myself, that's why, maybe, I carry them to other extremes than my predecessors. In other words, in the complications of society as we know it today, sometimes a person who can cut through the bureaucracy and red tape — even if I'm playing in a modern film — a person who thinks on that level is a hero. A person who can do that . . . a man who thinks on a very simple level and has very simple moral values appeals to a great many people."

One of the people who found the Eastwood character most appealing was Don Siegel. Siegel's view of the world bore close similarities to Eastwood's, and with *Coogan's Bluff* the director found a star whose image and attitude were the perfect vehicle for his own directorial ambitions. Theirs was a partnership made in heaven. "He's got that indefinable something that is the best in America. We sorta look up to him," Siegel says. "He's cleancut, he's strong, he's resolute, he's honest. I don't mean to be saccharine about it or fatuous about it, but he's the kind of chap that, certainly at my age, I'd like my son to turn out like."

Siegel entered Hollywood in 1934. By 1946 he was making features. He is a survivor, one of the last great individualists in a system dominated by the studios and finance houses. His heroes, like his own view of himself, are outsiders whose strength derives from the integrity of their vision and the skill with which they execute it. His films are economical and tightly structured. Within a modest framework he is capable of producing films which entertain and provoke. Whilst acknowledging the pressures of commercial demands he has carved out a personal style

which he uses, where possible, to convey a personal view of a world in which his heroes reproduce his own struggles against a crippling and harmful authoritarianism.

Siegel carried that view through the shifting patterns of the post-war world. He felt himself to be "A prophet without honour", but the late sixties and the seventies were his time. The world had gelled into a bureaucratised rigidity. Siegel's increasingly romanticised obsession with the individual and an individual morality may have been profoundly reactionary, but at least he identified the right enemy for the mass of people in the 'civilised world'.

Riot In Cell Block II (1954) was a decisive point in Siegel's career, setting the basic pattern for many of his films to come. Siegel's approach to action films (the staple product of the Warners studio where Siegel was working) came under two distinct influences. Essentially for financial reasons, *Riot In Cell Block II* was conceived as an action film pared down to the bone. Added to that was the producer Walter Wanger's aim to make a film attacking the prison system from a liberal position (Wanger had recently been gaoled). In the course of making a film to these requirements Siegel created the first of many "economical action films revealing a persistent ten-

sion with liberalism" (so described in Alan Lovell's pamphlet on Don Siegel).

The typical Siegel hero seems to marry two identities. He (it is always a man) appears as both a crusader against evil and a superman struggling against the tides of change. Superficially the liberal crusader and the conservative superman live in an harmonious unity, but the demands of social realism created tensions in this marriage. It began to show all the signs of an irretrievable breakdown.

The American crime film contains one of the richest veins of social realism in contemporary culture, and by the mid-sixties social realism had to

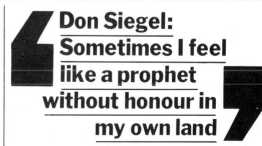

Don Siegel: Sometimes I feel like a prophet without honour in my own land

come to terms with a growing unease at the whittling away of democratic process in the western world.

Conservatism was suspect, liberalism seemed inadequate and any hero who was meant to keep the two together had to be placed under a threat of exaggerated proportions. Added to that was an increasing feeling in the movie industry that the 'cinema of excess' was the only available weapon with which to win audiences away from television.

The rogue-cop story offered the best solution to the problem of finding a crime film for the age. The ingredients were just right — authority refined into bureaucracy; monstrous criminals; people who didn't just dominate but exploited and manipulated as well; personalities fragmented into types; violent conflicts drawn out of oppressive tensions; a pinch of sex and a larger dollop of the new social background. In the rogue-cop story society is a battleground and the hero is the last great individual. For Siegel he became the only character who could maintain the double identity of liberal crusader and conservative superman.

Siegel's first big-budget box-office success was about just such a man. *Madigan* (1967) features Richard Widmark as the rogue. Harry Guardino plays his partner — a sort of liberal conscience.

Don Siegel: There's only one way to get into pictures if you have as little talent as I have: you have to know somebody

There is a corrupt chief inspector, a weak and compromised police commissioner; a black minister who spends most of the picture alleging police brutality; Madigan's ambitious wife; the commissioner's mistress; and, of course, a vicious killer. At the end of the film, Madigan and the killer die in a shoot-out, but the film ends on a note of cautious optimism when the commissioner and the chief inspector accept personal responsibility for their follies and agree to take a constructive approach in sorting out the mess.

Interestingly, it is this positive approach to the failings of the bureaucracy that must have appealed to Eastwood as much as Siegel's talent for action directing and his concern with the heroic outsider. Eastwood's image, in turn, was exactly right for the part of Siegel's late sixties hero.

Eastwood came to *Coogan's Bluff* because he owed Universal a picture. At the time he came into the project, however, not even a final script had been agreed. The scheduled director, Alex Segal, came off the picture when he failed to find a satisfactory script. Eastwood's advice on a possible replacement was sought. Don Taylor was considered and rejected, a number of other possibles were put forward, but Siegel was the one director whose earlier work impressed everybody.

Siegel viewed Eastwood's Italian westerns before agreeing to work on the project. The director and star first met in the office of Universal's vice-president in charge of features, Jennings Lang. The meeting was unremarkable and the two 'prophets without honour' parted — Eastwood to work on other projects, Siegel to sort out a usable script.

Siegel's first script for *Coogan's Bluff* (written by Jack Laird) was the ninth attempt. A tenth draft (by Howard Rodman) actually met with the approval of Siegel and Lang. Eastwood, however, threatened to pull out of the picture if it was used. Siegel became impatient. "I was insulted," he recalls. "The script I was responsible for was hated. But I also had a strange ambivalence and I thought, 'Thank God I'm off the picture'." At the time Siegel was working on another project that interested him more — a film called *The Other Man* also scripted by Howard Rodman. *The Other Man* never happened because Jennings Lang insisted that Eastwood and Siegel make *Coogan's Bluff*.

Eastwood was unaware of the existence of a number of early script drafts. When Siegel told him about them, the two of them pulled out four or five versions and, with the aid of writer Dean Reisner, cobbled together a final, satisfactory version.

Co-operation at this stage led to mutual admiration and close collaboration between the director and his star. Siegel found Eastwood "very knowledgeable about making pictures". He discovered that Eastwood's self-reliant image carried over into his professional attitudes. As an actor, according to Siegel, Eastwood "doesn't require, and I don't give him, too much direction". Despite, in Siegel's opinion, a tendency to underestimate his range as an actor, "Clint knows what he's doing when he acts and when he picks the material". But before that, Siegel found Eastwood to be one of the rare breed of actors whose interest in the directorial process was both obvious and helpful. "He started to come up with ideas for camera set-ups," says Siegel. "I started to call these Clintus shots and even if I decided not to use them, they invariably gave me another idea, threw me into a Siegelini shot."

Eastwood, in turn, comments on Siegel: "He's straightforward and knows what he wants. He never gets bogged down even in a disaster, and he likes to hear ideas. He has an ego like everyone else, but if a janitor comes up with something Don won't turn it down. He breeds an atmosphere of participation."

Leone emerges from Eastwood's comments as something of a gloriously inspired but chaotic egotist. Siegel, on the other hand, appears to be a disciplined, but democratic, leader. Working with Siegel seems to have provided the very atmosphere in which Eastwood's talents could take shape and grow. The partnership was remarkably fruitful and rewarding.

Despite all the complications and difficulties — the rejected scripts; arguments between director and producer, director and star, star and producer; a rigid and very tight shooting schedule; and, to cap it all, wintry conditions on location in the Mojave Desert and New York — the shooting on *Coogan's*

Bluff was finished in time for Christmas, 1967, and the film was an artistic and commercial success. It opened in mid-1968 and by the end of that year Eastwood was the fifth biggest box-office star in the USA after Sidney Poitier, Paul Newman, Julie Andrews and John Wayne.

Eastwood saw in 1968 en route to Austria for the filming of *Where Eagles Dare*. It was the beginning of a year of hard work, leading to exceptional rewards. By 1971 it was estimated that Eastwood's films had grossed around $200 million. He was the world's top box-office star.

PROFITS WITH EVEN LESS?

If Clint Eastwood takes great pains to keep his personal and professional lives separate, his professional life itself contains two independent but at times confused elements. As well as an artist (whether as actor or director), Eastwood is also a businessman. He has, in fact, bought a considerable degree of artistic independence with the awards won by some astute business deals. But before that, he succeeded in building a business (and, consequently, a secure financial position for himself and his family) through some crafty exploitation of his artistry.

The two or three years at the end of the sixties were perhaps Eastwood's most active and fruitful period. But they are years in which artist, businessman and private individual are intertwined in what seems an unruly tangle. We should start with Malpaso.

Eastwood's concern with managing his financial affairs and his artistic commitments is clear from as far back as the Rawhide days, when he came into conflict with CBS TV over the exclusivity of his contract and over his directorial ambitions. By 1968, he had made enough money to start thinking in terms of setting up his own company. There are certain financial advantages in being a highly paid actor effectively operating as an employee of a production company. Probably more important to Eastwood was the freedom such a company offered him in setting up, financing and overseeing the projects he wanted to be involved in. His experiences with Universal in the early days and with RKO and CBS TV no doubt encouraged Eastwood to appreciate the benefits of independence.

Malpaso (named after a piece of property owned by the Eastwood family, the word means 'bad step' or 'bad pass' in Spanish) was formed, according to Eastwood, directly after *The Beguiled* had been made (1970) — although the name appears on the production company credits for *Hang 'Em High*, *Two Mules for Sister Sara* and *The Beguiled* itself. This is because although Eastwood was involved in the production of these early films, the company itself did not yet exist.

Malpaso is a small scale operation, involving four people directly — Eastwood, Robert Daley, a script editor and a secretary. Daley was a man after East-

wood's own heart, "a producer in the old sense" who oversees the financing and the actual production of a film rather than one who "buys a story, puts their name on it and resells it". Equally important, Daley was (and is) concerned to cut the cost of film-making, or at least to make the process more efficient and more cost-effective. This goes some way to explaining the financial basis of Eastwood's success — he doesn't waste money. Malpaso's films are tightly budgeted and as tightly scheduled. Eastwood is a fast director, like Siegel, and also like Siegel he believes in 'covering lean' (that is shooting as little film as necessary before cutting). As an actor he likes, if anything, to over-rehearse scenes in front

of the camera. Sometimes a particularly inspired piece of improvisation is lost this way — but the familiarity with the lines, movements and geography of the scene that is developed does save time, film and money.

Eastwood began setting up Malpaso almost as soon as he began making films in America in 1967. His eventual partner, Robert Daley, had been at Universal in the fifties — first as a cost analyst and later as a unit manager — and for some time Malpaso was closely identified with Universal. The Malpaso office was on the Universal lot in Hollywood and most Malpaso films were co-produced and distributed by Universal. But Eastwood gradu-

ally became unhappy with Universal's publicity and distribution machine and with *The Outlaw Josey Wales* the company moved permanently to Warner Brothers. The identification with a particular major studio has never been total, and Eastwood has wisely allowed Malpaso to hire him out to other studios.

However, at the end of 1968 Eastwood was still only a rising star. 1969 and most of 1970 were spent consolidating a growing hold on the box office. For what were presumably the twin aims of widening his reputation and earning enough money to enable him to set-up his own company and carry out his own projects, Eastwood made a series of big-budget blockbusters. These would be widely shown, reaching audiences who may never have been aware of Eastwood before, and accordingly they involved the actor in uncharacteristic roles. It's a measure of Eastwood's wisdom that when the first blockbuster, *Where Eagles Dare*, was made it featured him in second billing to Richard Burton, but today the film is advertised and known as a Clint Eastwood picture.

Where Eagles Dare is a two and a half hour long adventure film. Scripted by Alistair MacLean from his own novel, it is a typical World War II thriller firmly within the sub-genre MacLean has made his own. Stars and locations apart it is virtually indistinguishable from any of the other MacLean novels/films — *Guns Of Navarone*, *Ice Station Zebra*, *Puppet On A Chain* or *When Eight Bells Toll*. All of these are among a considerable number of similar wartime espionage epics made in the late sixties with a greater or lesser degree of inventiveness and wit. Their purpose was to win audiences away from the home comforts of television and, by and large, they succeeded admirably.

The technique was simplicity itself — spend a lot of money, employ a number of big money making stars and set the action in visually stunning locations (for the sake of American audiences these were usually in Europe). Unlike earlier war films, the blockbusters were most comfortable ignoring the political, psychological and moral complications of war.

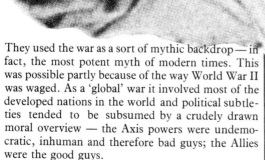

They used the war as a sort of mythic backdrop — in fact, the most potent myth of modern times. This was possible partly because of the way World War II was waged. As a 'global' war it involved most of the developed nations in the world and political subtleties tended to be subsumed by a crudely drawn moral overview — the Axis powers were undemocratic, inhuman and therefore bad guys; the Allies were the good guys.

This simplistic morality is implicit in *Where Eagles Dare*, as in other films of its kind. It replaces any other, more difficult, plot dynamic — conflict is

always in terms of this presupposed fight between good and evil with spies, double-agents and resulting twists in plot providing the necessary spice. The war offers other ingredients for the mythic mix — scenes of violence and destruction on a vast scale, a backdrop sufficiently familiar and recent to be recognisable and yet far enough away in time to allow imagination some scope. *Where Eagles Dare* is the sort of film that convinces on its own level by providing a fictional 'secret history' of an event in which large numbers of people were totally involved in tiny areas of the whole. The war affected everybody but most of them knew little about its grand strategy and overall operation and the passage of time has worn away even their limited memories.

Where Eagles Dare sees Clint Eastwood playing an American soldier who joins forces with a British Commando unit under Richard Burton. Their ostensible mission is to rescue an American general carrying important information from an impregnable fortress high in the Alps. Their actual mission is to uncover the secret network of Nazi spies operating within the domestic British intelligence agencies. Through a series of dramatic twists we discover that the general is, in fact, an actor masquerading as a general; that three members of the commando unit are Nazi agents; that Richard Burton is first an agent (good guy), then a double agent (bad guy), then a triple agent (good guy); that the 'Mr Big' of the Nazi agents is the head of MI5. The Germans are invariably bad, the British invariably good and Eastwood is allowed a few minutes of unremitting and almost totally mechanical killing.

Of course, it's pure hokum. There is no characterisation, no sub-plots and hardly any plot. The story moves in a series of computerised episodes to the 'chase' (the escape from the fortress) and the final, banally executed denouement. Such films are strangely unsatisfying, like a perfunctory sexual encounter. Everything that makes the event special is absent except the climax, and in order to carry its audience along the films (and the original stories) desperately strive to effect as many climaxes as possible within the allotted time. In the late sixties, though, nothing succeeded in the cinema like excess. Or, to put it another way, the film's main weapon in the ratings war against television was size and money. Screen dimensions, running time, the number of stars per square inch, the number of special effects per second — these were the things that were thought to matter. For a while the tactic worked well. The films made money. They reduced the cinematic art to its bare essentials and magnified those essentials to huge proportions. The films, like economy-sized detergents, gave audiences value for money. Audiences reciprocated by allowing themselves to be overawed by the scale of the things. It was quite easy to see the simplicity of the exposition as clarity and the plot twists as profundity.

In some ways, *Where Eagles Dare* fits with Eastwood's ideas about cinema. Certainly it presents him as a self-sufficient character, a man with no name. But only because it presents him as a totally mechanical character, not even questioning a conventional

cinematic portrayal of morality — as Leone did with the western. Lt. Shaeffer in *Where Eagles Dare* is, like all the other characters, a mere prop. It seems likely that Eastwood saw *Where Eagles Dare* as little more than money in the bank and a route to a wider audience. Certainly he belittles his own role by persistently referring to this epic as *Where Doubles Dare*.

Curiously, the portrayal of Shaeffer diverges from his character in the novel. Even the harshest critic of Eastwood's acting talent would accept that he could act the part with his eyes closed and both hands tied behind his back. Yet some effort has clearly been made to create out of the Shaeffer character a role appropriate to the Eastwood image. Brian G. Hutton, the director of *Where Eagles Dare* (and of Eastwood's later MGM blockbuster *Kelly's Heroes*) explained:

"I think we went twenty years of film from 1947, when Brando hit, until 1967 when Clint hit, with actors who for the most part played characters who were confused. Now Clint is a throwback to the strong, silent men of the 1930s. Clint's character has

> ## To me love for a person is respect for individual feelings – respecting privacy and accepting faults

always been a guy who knows where he is, knows what he wants and goes out and does it. Regardless if he's good or bad, at least he's certain."

In *Where Eagles Dare* Shaeffer is revealed to be a professional assassin, the legitimate heir to No Name. Hutton's comments suggest why this bequest was made. Unlike Newman, MacQueen or Nicholson, audiences do not see Eastwood's characters as extensions of himself. On the contrary, like Bogart, Cagney and Gary Cooper, they see him as an extension of his characters. You don't identify with Eastwood, you emulate him or desire him. This means that the perceptive film-maker will cast Eastwood in a role which confirms the qualities his other characters display. He does not have the flexibility of a number of his contemporaries, who, finding themselves in an unlikely cinematic situation, can carry off the portrayal simply by seeming to be themselves. Siegel suggests that Eastwood underestimates his range as an actor, but experience has shown that some parts he undertakes are measureably less successful than others. A singing Eastwood, for example, is no more palatable to the average cinemagoer than would be Bogart in red-nose and a clown costume.

However, like any true Hollywood star of the great era, Eastwood's acting ambitions have often taken him in curious directions. A singing Clint is

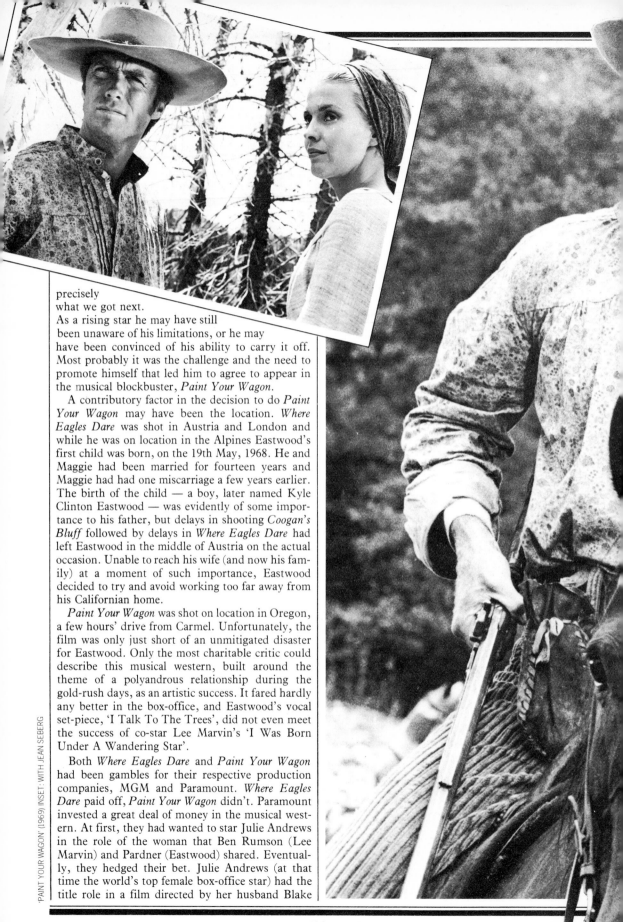

precisely
what we got next.
As a rising star he may have still
been unaware of his limitations, or he may
have been convinced of his ability to carry it off.
Most probably it was the challenge and the need to
promote himself that led him to agree to appear in
the musical blockbuster, *Paint Your Wagon*.

A contributory factor in the decision to do *Paint
Your Wagon* may have been the location. *Where
Eagles Dare* was shot in Austria and London and
while he was on location in the Alpines Eastwood's
first child was born, on the 19th May, 1968. He and
Maggie had been married for fourteen years and
Maggie had had one miscarriage a few years earlier.
The birth of the child — a boy, later named Kyle
Clinton Eastwood — was evidently of some importance to his father, but delays in shooting *Coogan's
Bluff* followed by delays in *Where Eagles Dare* had
left Eastwood in the middle of Austria on the actual
occasion. Unable to reach his wife (and now his family) at a moment of such importance, Eastwood
decided to try and avoid working too far away from
his Californian home.

Paint Your Wagon was shot on location in Oregon,
a few hours' drive from Carmel. Unfortunately, the
film was only just short of an unmitigated disaster
for Eastwood. Only the most charitable critic could
describe this musical western, built around the
theme of a polyandrous relationship during the
gold-rush days, as an artistic success. It fared hardly
any better in the box-office, and Eastwood's vocal
set-piece, 'I Talk To The Trees', did not even meet
the success of co-star Lee Marvin's 'I Was Born
Under A Wandering Star'.

Both *Where Eagles Dare* and *Paint Your Wagon*
had been gambles for their respective production
companies, MGM and Paramount. *Where Eagles
Dare* paid off, *Paint Your Wagon* didn't. Paramount
invested a great deal of money in the musical western. At first, they had wanted to star Julie Andrews
in the role of the woman that Ben Rumson (Lee
Marvin) and Pardner (Eastwood) shared. Eventually, they hedged their bet. Julie Andrews (at that
time the world's top female box-office star) had the
title role in a film directed by her husband Blake

Edwards, *Darlin' Lili*, and Jean Seberg got the part of Elizabeth in *Paint Your Wagon*. Unfortunately for Paramount, neither of the films made the sort of profits they needed. The two greatest hopes to restore Paramount's ailing health were both universally described as flops. Paramount nearly went out of business.

Nevertheless, the companies still tried hard and with *Where Eagles Dare* and *Paint Your Wagon* in the can, the press junketing began. For a year or more Eastwood commuted between London, Paris, Rome, California and various locations. He went accompanied by press agents and PRs. He gave interviews in hotel rooms, on set and at premieres. The golden boy was being turned into a household name.

Eastwood got more than just a great deal of publicity out of his association with Paramount and MGM. He learnt about the risks involved in selling

> ## My personal life . . . I just don't care to have it exploited. I get no satisfaction out of having it exploited

yourself to a studio bent on creating a money making vehicle in which you are just another big name. Sometimes it worked out. In *Where Eagles Dare* Eastwood found a sympathetic director and a story that even the most determined interference from studio big-wigs could not ruin. A fifties musical — even one as good as Alan Jay Lerner and Frederick Loewe's *Paint Your Wagon* (they had written *My Fair Lady*) — was a different matter.

Eastwood's comments about *Where Eagles Dare* and *Paint Your Wagon* are instructive. "It was a very strange script," he says of the former, "with lots of exposition. Even the character I played had tremendous amounts of exposition — we'd stop and talk for hours about what's gonna happen . . . The director and I felt that that was very impractical, and so we let Richard's character handle the exposition. He has a beautiful speaking voice and he's very good at that kind of thing. And I would handle the shooting which they thought I was very good at."

Paint Your Wagon, on the other hand, "wasn't the most smooth-running picture I've ever been on . . . I saw that film in four (sic) different versions — the director's version, the producer's version and then the coalition of all the studio execs and their version, and of all the versions the director's, the first one, was actually the best one. But that wasn't the one that was released."

Eastwood realised that it wasn't good enough just to be involved in the decision making. "I wanted control", he says. Soon after the release of *Paint Your Wagon*, Malpaso Productions went into business.

'KELLY'S HEROES' (1970) INSET: WITH DONALD SUTHERLAND

While filming *Where Eagles Dare* near Salzburg, Eastwood became friendly with Richard Burton. Burton's inconstant companion, Liz Taylor, stayed with the unit for much of the time and she told Eastwood of her next project — a film called *Two Mules For Sister Sara* that was based on a Budd Boetticher story. Taylor suggested that he might be interested in playing the role opposite her — Hogan to her Sara. Eastwood read the script and agreed. Universal agreed that the casting would be good and Eastwood flew off to Mexico in the spring of 1969.

In the event, Liz Taylor was unavailable and Eastwood found himself playing opposite Shirley MacLaine. The partnership was not a happy one.

For one thing, Eastwood felt she was wrong for the part of a brothel madame masquerading as a nun — "her casting stretched the imagination a bit and required some rewriting". For another, MacLaine's well-known liberal views and Eastwood's conservative anarchism didn't mix too well. And then, MacLaine played the star bit, eating in her caravan and flying back to the city whenever she wasn't needed, while Eastwood stayed in the nearby village of Tlayacapan and mucked in with the crew. He soon learnt, but playing the star didn't come easy.

One partnership on *Two Mules For Sister Sara* was happy. The film marked the second collaboration

between Eastwood and Don Siegel and while Siegel had problems himself with producer Marty Rackin, under his expert eye the film succeeded well enough. It took sixty-five days to shoot — entirely on location — and the budget was over $4 million, small by the standard set by *Where Eagles Dare* and *Paint Your Wagon* but a considerable increase on the Italian westerns.

No sooner had Eastwood finished shooting *Two Mules For Sister Sara* than he was off to Yugoslavia to begin work on *The Warriors* (eventually released as *Kelly's Heroes*). One project — a film about a Chicago gambler, *Cully The Arm* — had been shelved and *Kelly's Heroes* was probably a wiser bet.

It was another MGM blockbuster, this time co-produced and co-financed by a Yugoslavian company, and it set the seal on Eastwood's box-office drawing power. By the end of 1970, when *Kelly's Heroes* was released, Eastwood was the second biggest draw in the US.

Kelly's Heroes repeated the *Where Eagles Dare* formula with the important difference that the former film belonged to the *Dirty Dozen* school of lighthearted wartime thrillers and bore only a marginal relationship to the straightforward adventure stories purveyed by such as Alistair MacLean. Both films had the director, Brian G. Hutton, in common and both made generous use of spectacular visuals and the wartime landscape of destruction, but *Kelly's Heroes* was played definitely tongue-in-cheek and the combined efforts of Eastwood and his co-star Donald Sutherland resulted in some notable moments of relaxed comedy.

The story, briefly, puts Eastwood at the head of an American platoon in Italy towards the end of World War II. The platoon hit upon the idea of enlivening the war and, under the cover of battle, they rob a bank. It's an amusing story of unexceptional qualities, but the combination of thriller and wartime adventure (with a pinch of comedy) had proved to be attractive to audiences. Like *Where Eagles Dare* and *Paint Your Wagon* it lasted well over two hours and provided a cheap and undemanding evening's entertainment.

Clearly, Eastwood had not made *Paint Your Wagon* for the money alone. He received an advance of $250,000 for that film while he had already been paid $400,000 plus 25% of net takings for *Hang 'Em High*. If experience and promotion had been the main concerns with *Where Eagles Dare*, *Paint Your Wagon* and *Kelly's Heroes* by the time Eastwood made *Kelly's Heroes* he was quite capable of being paid on the very top scale as well. A figure of $750,000 advance was being bandied about during the planning of *Kelly's Heroes*, and that plus a percentage no doubt brought home more than the fabled million dollars per picture. Clint Eastwood was flying high.

SEX AND THE SINGLE MAN

In some ways, *Two Mules For Sister Sara* saw the return of the familiar Eastwood cowboy character. But only in some ways. *Hang 'Em High* and *Coogan's Bluff* gave the rootless westerner sexual liaisons if not actual sexual attachments or personal commitments. *Two Mules For Sister Sara* ends with a picture of the cowboy, Hogan, as a marriage partner — or rather, as a caricature of a husband in a parody of a marriage. In this film and in the two following *Kelly's Heroes* (*The Beguiled* and *Play 'Misty' For Me* — the first Malpaso production proper and Eastwood's first film as a director) women play vastly more significant parts than in any of Eastwood's previous movies.

There are, of course, sound commercial reasons for introducing women/sex into Eastwood's films. What is more important is that the introduction of women and an overt and elaborate sexual dimension reveals a broadening out of the Eastwood character. In the real world there is sex. In the mythic world that No Name inhabited there was no need for it. The interesting question, then, is what *kind* of sexual being does No Name become.

Two Mules For Sister Sara is set in Mexico during the 1860s. Maximilian has been installed by the French as emperor, and the Mexican people under Juares are engaged in a successful struggle against occupying French forces. An itinerant cowboy (Hogan) comes upon three men about to rape a

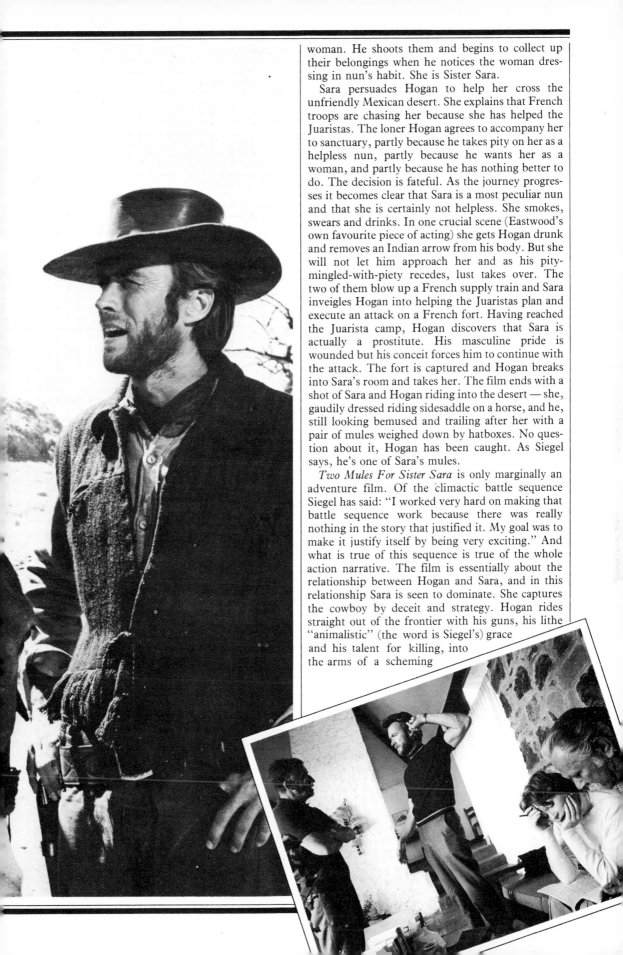

woman. He shoots them and begins to collect up their belongings when he notices the woman dressing in nun's habit. She is Sister Sara.

Sara persuades Hogan to help her cross the unfriendly Mexican desert. She explains that French troops are chasing her because she has helped the Juaristas. The loner Hogan agrees to accompany her to sanctuary, partly because he takes pity on her as a helpless nun, partly because he wants her as a woman, and partly because he has nothing better to do. The decision is fateful. As the journey progresses it becomes clear that Sara is a most peculiar nun and that she is certainly not helpless. She smokes, swears and drinks. In one crucial scene (Eastwood's own favourite piece of acting) she gets Hogan drunk and removes an Indian arrow from his body. But she will not let him approach her and as his pity-mingled-with-piety recedes, lust takes over. The two of them blow up a French supply train and Sara inveigles Hogan into helping the Juaristas plan and execute an attack on a French fort. Having reached the Juarista camp, Hogan discovers that Sara is actually a prostitute. His masculine pride is wounded but his conceit forces him to continue with the attack. The fort is captured and Hogan breaks into Sara's room and takes her. The film ends with a shot of Sara and Hogan riding into the desert — she, gaudily dressed riding sidesaddle on a horse, and he, still looking bemused and trailing after her with a pair of mules weighed down by hatboxes. No question about it, Hogan has been caught. As Siegel says, he's one of Sara's mules.

Two Mules For Sister Sara is only marginally an adventure film. Of the climactic battle sequence Siegel has said: "I worked very hard on making that battle sequence work because there was really nothing in the story that justified it. My goal was to make it justify itself by being very exciting." And what is true of this sequence is true of the whole action narrative. The film is essentially about the relationship between Hogan and Sara, and in this relationship Sara is seen to dominate. She captures the cowboy by deceit and strategy. Hogan rides straight out of the frontier with his guns, his lithe "animalistic" (the word is Siegel's) grace and his talent for killing, into the arms of a scheming

WITH SHIRLEY MACLAINE IN 'TWO MULES FOR SISTER SARA' (1970)

woman. If you wanted to know why No Name never had a woman the answer is here. He can survive any depredation, any attack except the onslaught of the determined female. He makes one mistake, admits one weakness — he agrees to help a woman — and is done for. It's a profoundly sexist view, not because it diminishes women but because it sees them as posing an exaggerated threat to masculinity. Eastwood's characters see all personal relationships as potentially dangerous, because they create chinks in a private armour. They see sexual relationships as emasculating. Hogan is even allowed to make his mistake because he thinks Sara is a nun — that is, a non-woman. See how deceptive appearances can be! See how the gunfighter must live by a code that is higher than mere reality!

Two Mules For Sister Sara is in some ways a peculiar film for Siegel to have made. It might be a footnote, a marginal comment on the alien nature of woman, almost a comedy in the manner of Clark Gable and Claudette Colbert, were it not for *The Beguiled*. If the hostile society so typical of Siegel films is replaced by an individual in *Two Mules For Sister Sara*, *The Beguiled* suggests that Sara might be more than just an individual — she might be the representative of a hostile society, the society of women.

The Beguiled is in Siegel's own estimation, his best picture. It's certainly the most self-consciously *artistic* film he's made and also, probably, the most tightly structured and craftily worked film he's made. But it represents a disturbing view of women and one that confirms many of the characteristics of the Eastwood male persona.

"One reason I wanted to do the picture," says Siegel, "is that it's a woman's picture, not a picture for women, but about them. Women are capable of deceit, larceny, murder, anything. Behind that mask of innocence lurks just as much evil as you'll find in members of the Mafia. Any young girl, who looks perfectly harmless, is capable of murder."

The Beguiled was shot entirely on location in New Orleans. It took some ten weeks of filming and Eastwood received the comparatively low sum of $600,000. The film was a labour of love. Eastwood was given the story whilst visiting Hollywood during a break in the shooting of *Two Mules For Sister Sara*. He liked it and gave it to Siegel to read. By the time Siegel agreed to do it, Eastwood was having doubts about his suitability for the part. Siegel argued that while adventure parts were ten-a-penny, a film like *The Beguiled* came by once in a lifetime. It was a risk, but Universal, who owned the book, were agreeable and in late 1969, while Eastwood was filming *Kelly's Heroes* Don Siegel set to work on research, casting, scripting and all the other preparation necessary before an inch of film can be shot.

The Beguiled opens to the sounds of the American Civil War. Black and white photographs of the war give way to a sepia wash as the film proper starts. A little girl is picking mushrooms in a forest. Voices singing 'When Johnny Comes Marching Home' give way to a fragile solo voice — Eastwood singing the mournful 'Don't Go For A Soldier'. The girl spots a wounded soldier propped up against a tree. As the camera picks out the soldier's blood-soaked foot, the sepia gives way to full colour.

The soldier, Johnny McBurney (Eastwood), is taken to the girls' seminary from where the child had come. He is a Union soldier who has been left behind Southern lines as the battle moved on. Nevertheless, he is a wounded man and the two women who run the seminary — Martha Farnsworth (Geraldine Page) and Edwina Dabney (Elizabeth Hartman) — decide to care for him. They lock him in his room, bathe him, dress him and nurse him. They try to keep him away from the girls, but one of them — Carol (Jo Ann Harris) — is old enough to have her own ideas.

While McBurney is still recuperating, a Confederate patrol passes the school. Martha decides not to turn him over to them, saying that she doesn't think he's well enough. Through a series of flashbacks and dream sequences it becomes clear that McBurney has awakened strong sexual desires in both Martha and Edwina. His awareness of his own power is shown by his reactions when he hears of a certain Randolph living in the school. Randolph, however, turns out to be the pet turtle cared for by the girl who found McBurney.

McBurney is a beguiler. Seeing the seminary as a sort of sanctuary with optional extras he starts to play off one female against the others. He even 'seduces' the slave helper Hallie (Mae Mercer). One night, while deciding whether he should grace Martha or Edwina first, Carol draws him to her room. It is a moment of weakness when the young girl's untrammelled sexuality is more appealing than the survival game he is playing with Martha and Edwina's repressions. He and Carol wake Edwina

'Don Siegel: The Beguiled is a yarn about a man who zigged when he should have zagged'

unwittingly and, in a fury of unrequited lust, she runs after McBurney and throws him downstairs. His leg is severely broken and Martha decides that it must be amputated. This has the added advantage of making McBurney helpless — symbolically castrating him.

McBurney's anger is uncontrollable when he discovers that the women have removed his leg. He humiliates Martha by revealing that she once had an incestuous relationship with her brother, and he kills Randolph. He threatens to turn the women in to a nearby company of Union soldiers. Edwina takes pity on him and follows him to his room to console him. Martha and the girls, meanwhile, decide that like a wounded animal he is too dangerous to live. They prepare a meal for him, knowing that he loves mushrooms, using poisonous toadstools picked by the little girl.

When he comes down for dinner, he apologises for his outburst and announces that he and Edwina are to be married. In a moment of high tension in which the camera travels round the faces at the table, Martha and the girls watch as McBurney guzzles into a plateful of 'mushrooms'. They are the beguilers now. McBurney dies as the women finish

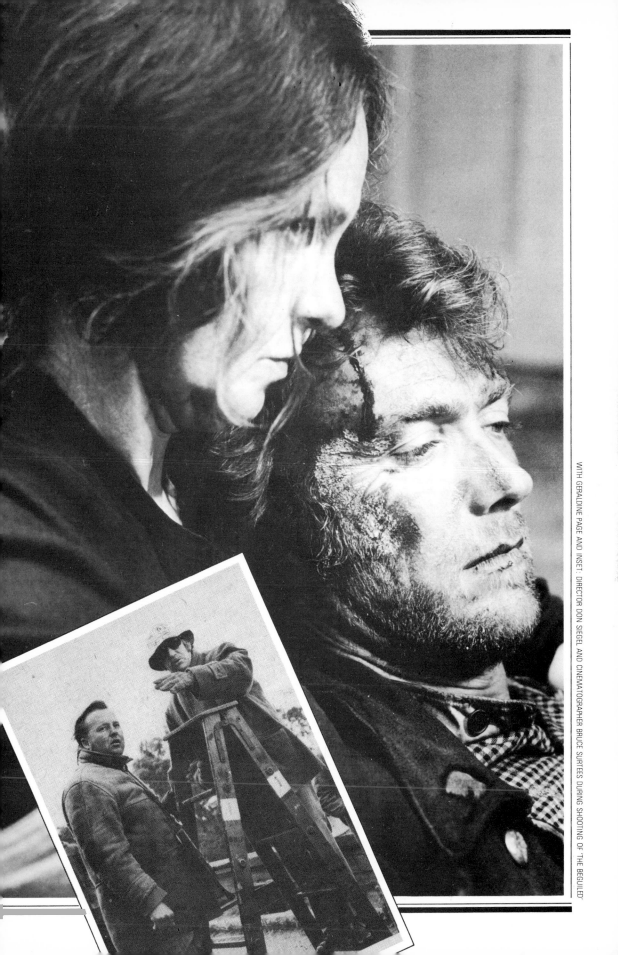

WITH GERALDINE PAGE AND INSET: DIRECTOR DON SIEGEL AND CINEMATOGRAPHER BRUCE SURTEES DURING SHOOTING OF 'THE BEGUILED'

their meal.

The final sequence shows the women carrying McBurney's body outside to be buried in the school grounds. The plaintive 'Don't Go For A Soldier' returns to the soundtrack and the film turns monochrome again for the final credits.

The Beguiled is a beautifully built film. Siegel's careful use of imagery works to convey a feeling of doom-laden claustrophobia of almost Gothic dimensions. The photography (for the first time under the direction of Bruce Surtees who was later to work on all the Eastwood directed movies) is nothing short of exquisite. And, of course, the implications are clear — McBurney is a free spirit brought down by "this monstrous regiment of women". He is the crow which you see in the film, chained and held captive by "a little covey of sparrows" (one of the many alternative titles mooted for the film was *A Nest Of Sparrows*).

Yet, *The Beguiled* is not a simple-minded film. McBurney's arrival does not just mean the intrusion of a superior masculinity into a feminine world. Nor does he simply represent the strong individual struggling against a collective of weaklings. He is essentially a symbol of pain and its necessary physicality. When the women bury McBurney, they reject the presence of pain and they repress their own sexuality. It's McBurney's blood which brings

" Jennings Lang (on The Beguiled): Maybe a lot of people just don't want to see Clint Eastwood's leg cut off "

colour to the scene. His physical vulnerability is a vitalising force and his death and burial represents the victory of the superego.

McBurney is not brutal in himself. He, like Coogan, Harry Callahan, Marshall Duncan or Josey Wales, is like an animal brutalised by civilisation itself. With his burial, life — and all civilised life is history — returns to its dull sepia-toned uniformity.

There is much validity in the view that sexuality and pain are linked through an acceptance of physicality. The Eastwood character, however, sees sexuality as a social relationship in a society which he rejects. The positive version of the equation between sexuality and pain is seen in other Eastwood films where social power (the ability of the individual to influence society) is equated with sexual potency. In the Dirty Harry films especially the phallic symbolism of Eastwood's weapon is inescapable, and while the sexuality-pain equation is superficially plausible, the equation between social power and sexual potency is positively attractive. It offers a magical clarity in a murky world where social issues are complex and confused and sexual roles are questioned by a new awareness.

The problem is that while audiences can detect solutions in the Eastwood character, they are fantastic solutions because they only refer, if at all, to unreal questions. Thus *Dirty Harry* — the most violently received of all Eastwood's films — presupposes a villain of horror-film proportions. Such villains do exist and a real life Harry Callahan's behaviour would be understandable if problematic. But Siegel and Eastwood (at least until *The Outlaw Josey Wales*) intentionally ignore the conditions which allow him to exist. As Siegel says of *Dirty Harry*, "I took the situation as it existed without going into the raison d'etre for the killer's action. I wasn't interested in his background. All I was interested in was that he was a killer." Criticism can be levelled because the film's social realism doesn't go far enough.

Eastwood is right when he says (as he often does) that he makes escapist films. He is right when he says, "A very self-sufficient human being is almost becoming a mythical character in our day and age." The attractiveness of the Eastwood character lies precisely in the desire we all share at times for self-sufficiency. Not to have to depend on others; not to be interfered with by others; not to be subject to an authority which we do not control — all these are common wants. *The Beguiled* places the Eastwood character in a situation where he cannot be self-sufficient. The hidden and dangerous assumption of the film is that such a situation is always threatening, and, where women are concerned, it destroys men and saps their masculinity.

It is a minor tragedy of modern life that a sexual relationship is commonly thought of as this sort of battleground. The individual who can command his or her feelings is then at an advantage, because victory means domination through a confirmation of sexual potency. Whenever Eastwood's characters give in to sexual temptation and admit their need, they lose. Or as Eastwood's co-star in *Coogan's Bluff*, Susan Clark, put it: "Part of [Eastwood's] sex appeal is the constant mystery — how deeply does he feel? How deeply is he involved in life?"

The Beguiled was released in summer, 1970. It was a box-office flop. Eastwood himself blamed Universal who distributed it and publicised it as if it were a predictable adventure film. After a disastrous Hollywood premiere, Universal had second thoughts and allowed the film to open in smaller 'arty' theatres. There, and especially in Europe where Siegel was highly thought of, the film began to attract a cult following. In subsequent years it went into profit, but Eastwood was sorely disappointed at the way Universal had treated the film. He was

CLINT WITH JESSICA WALTER (EVELYN) IN 'PLAY MISTY FOR ME' (1971)

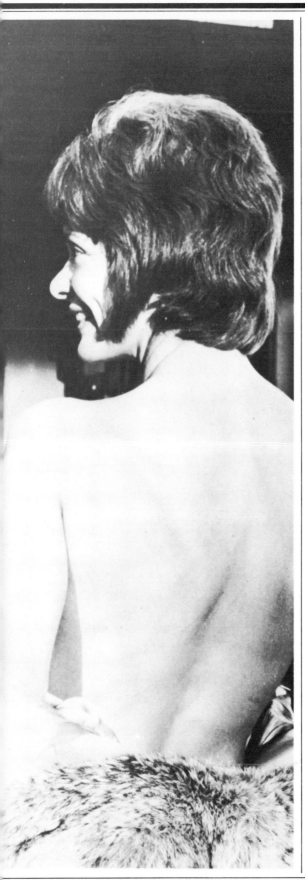

determined that Malpaso would guide his career from then on, and despite Universal's objections that the public would never buy Clint Eastwood as a disc jockey he decided to make *Play 'Misty' For Me* from a script he had sent to Universal some years previously. Universal would still distribute the picture, but it would be Malpaso's baby. That must have been something of a relief for Universal's vice-president in charge of features, Jennings Lang, who had argued that *The Beguiled* itself, and not the studio, was to blame for its commercial failure. "Maybe," he had said, "a lot of people don't want to see Clint Eastwood's leg cut off."

Play 'Misty' For Me was shot in and around Eastwood's home town of Carmel, California. The story was written by a woman friend of the Eastwoods, Jo Heims, who also wrote *Breezy,* and many critics

> **Jessica Walter: Clint Eastwood is not insecure or nervous. He doesn't impose things on you, he left the role up to me. He has faith in people (and) a wonderful calm strength that was very reassuring**

have wondered at the sentimentality of these two films. *Play 'Misty' For Me* features Eastwood as a late-night dee-jay, Dave Garland, who receives a regular anonymous request to play Errol Garner's song 'Misty'. One morning he gets picked up in a bar by a strange woman, Evelyn Draper (Jessica Walter), and discovers that she is the source of the requests. A one-night stand turns into a regular thing and Dave begins to worry that Evelyn is getting too involved. When his girlfriend Tobie Williams (Donna Mills) returns from Europe, she decides to break off her relationship with Dave.

Dave tries to get Tobie back and when Evelyn threatens to move in he throws her out. She returns and attacks his housekeeper with a knife, destroying much of his house in the process. Evelyn is arrested, but she is soon released into psychiatric care. She seems to have disappeared, and Dave and Tobie begin to see each other again. Tobie, however, is an independent woman and lives in her own apartment with a series of ever-changing flat-mates. So when a new flat-mate moves in, Dave is unsuspecting. Evelyn has changed her name, but a request to play 'Misty' gives the game away and Dave realises that Evelyn is planning to kill Tobie. He drives to the apartment and confronts Evelyn. After a protracted struggle he overpowers her and she falls from the balcony of Tobie's apartment into the Pacific Ocean. Dave and Tobie hold each other. The nightmare is over and they can begin to live together.

The romantic finale is, in fact, just the other side of sexism. Tobie needs Dave, and the recognition of her weakness is the basis of their future relationship. Her independence is shown to be unworkable, but once again only in the face of an abnormal threat. *Play 'Misty' For Me* has been compared to Hitchcock and there are obvious points of comparison with *Psycho*. But while Hitchcock's characters have no point of reference outside the cinema, Eastwood has come to stand for a whole section of society. It is not always easy to accept an Eastwood film (whether as star, or, in this case, as star and director) as simply an engaging piece of hokum. His persona resonates too strongly in the world outside.

If Tobie starts out as symbolic of the independent woman, Evelyn is shown to be her totally dependent alter ego. By the end of the film, total dependence is revealed as a mask for total domination and independence gives way to submissiveness. This is the

Don Siegel: Clint doesn't require too much direction

choice that Eastwood seems to present for sexual relationships — adding in other films the possibility of being totally detached and just occasionally condescending to rape someone. In fact, the real choice for him is not between the independent and the dependent woman but between the dominant and the submissive woman. Independence, Eastwood seems to be arguing, is just an illusion that women suffer in order to avoid recognising that they are weaker than men.

It is to Eastwood's credit that *Play 'Misty' For Me* actually accepts sexuality as a part of life. Dave Garland is forced to make a choice about his relationships, and the conflicts arising out of the existence of alternatives provide the motor of the drama. But the choice is made under circumstances that can, without exaggeration, be described as psychotic. It is almost an axiom of Eastwood's view of the cinema that films must portray larger-than-life situations. Characters emerge from this dramatic stranglehold as caricatures, and although Eastwood might shrug and say "That's entertainment" there is a disturbing illusion of realism about many of his most worrying films. It's a realism of place and time (which is one thing that distinguishes *Play 'Misty' For Me* from *Psycho*) which reacts with conventional non-realistic characterisation in a potent mix. *Play 'Misty' For Me* is a simple film. Its promise has yet to be fulfilled, but interestingly Eastwood's development seems to suggest a more realistic approach to his characters (specifically in *The Outlaw Josey Wales*). Possibly his best work is yet to come and it might turn out to be his most realistic work, too.

'TO LIVE OUTSIDE THE LAW YOU MUST BE HONEST' (RULES RULE O.K.?)

Dirty Harry burst upon an unsuspecting world in 1971. Rogue-cop films were nothing new — this was Don Siegel's third. But there were differences. Harry Callahan's methods are not so much unorthodox as psychotic, and, although the death of his wife is nodded to by way of the cursory explanation, psychological depth and motivations are almost invisible. Walt Coogan, for example, suffers from a rather tritely expressed sense of his own responsibility for the death of a prisoner. Callahan isn't restrained by even such limited consciousness, let alone by a liberal conscience. He seems to be overly concerned with efficiency — as the thrusting young executive in some earlier Hollywood film might have been. He despises the weak, the obstructive and those he doesn't like — a petulant child with "the most powerful hand-gun in the world".

This was something of a change for Eastwood. In his previous seven films (from *Coogan's Bluff* to *Play 'Misty' For Me*), No Name's hyper-violence was moderated. Violence was presented either in the guise of sheer escapism or simply as a fact of life. Even No Name's orgies of killing had an element of what Eastwood describes as the "satiric" in them. Harry Callahan, though, is a modern day killer, a killer with a social role. And while he doesn't kill people just for kicks, he doesn't do it simply because it's necessary either. He does it with a kind of relish. Killing the villain gives Harry Callahan something like an orgasmic release after the increasing tension and delays of the preceding chase. Dirty Harry is definitely not cool.

It's to Siegel's credit that the very end of *Dirty Harry* is the climactic moment when Harry throws his badge away. For a cop like Harry Callahan, who appears to have no other reason for living, it's a moment of *supreme* resignation. After coitus, all animals are sad. Eastwood, on the other hand, refused to shoot that scene for three days — and this divergence of opinion is as significant as it sounds.

Most of the objections to *Dirty Harry* suggest that it is a fascist film, or at least that Harry himself is a fascist. Eastwood, not unnaturally, denies the accusation. "There's nothing like that in there," he says. "The guy was just a man who fought bureaucracy and a certain established kind of thing. Just because he did things a little unorthodox — that's the only way he knew how to handle it. He had so many hours to solve the case and, as far as he was concerned, he was more interested in the victim than the law. He says in the picture he is a man of high morals. That the law is wrong if this person (the killer) can be let off on a technicality like that. Well the laws are changing — they're always changing back and forth in the courts; the pendulum is always swinging back and forth, right and left. Once

in a while the court gets too loose at one end, too conservative on the other and it changes every ten years. We, as Americans, went to Nuremberg and convicted people who committed certain crimes because they didn't adhere to a higher morality. We convicted them on that basis — that they shouldn't have listened to the law of the land or their leaders at that time. They should have listened to their true morality. We sent them to jail on that basis. This is how it is with this man. Somebody told him this is the way it is, too bad, and he said: 'Well that's wrong, I can't adhere to that.' That isn't fascist; that's the opposite of fascism.''

The interesting thing about this defence is its understatement. The ''unorthodox'' methods of Harry Callahan, for example, include wilful disobedience, threats, and torture. The ''technicality'' on which Scorpio (the killer) is released is that he has been brutally manhandled by Harry. Scorpio, of course, is presented as a monstrous psychopath and if *Dirty Harry* had been a western there would have been hardly a murmur from liberal critics. It is not the violence they object to, but the apparent approval with which one of the fundamentals of the American (and British) legal system is disposed of when it becomes inconvenient — that all suspects are innocent until proven guilty. Denying that is but a hairsbreadth away from saying that some people

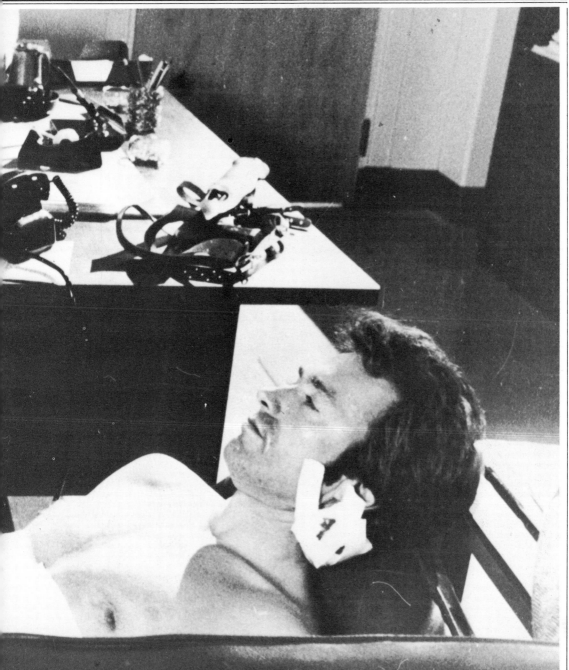

'DIRTY HARRY' (1971)

are guilty before they've even been arrested — and guilt can all too suddenly become not a matter of objective law, but the concern of private, subjective moralities.

In one sense, the problem is that Harry Callahan is an individualist in a world that has precious little time for individualists. He lives in civilised times when the gunman's private code has become society's public law. It's not that Harry Callahan and his ilk do their jobs efficiently as the licensed gunmen of the modern day. It's that their dedication to the law denies its civilised basis. They are undemocratic.

Interestingly, Harry Callahan can be seen as a symptom of a wider concern among some people about the alleged break-down of 'law and order' in society. This concern has been reflected (if not spearheaded) by all manner of media crime coverage. Perhaps the most notable area is television cop shows. A recent academic study in America has shown that in 1969 18.8% of TV cops made illegal searches and seizures, while 20.6% failed to advise their suspects of their rights. By 1971 these figures had risen to 55.4% and 50.8% respectively. And while this sort of phenomenon is often justified in terms of dramatic need (it's more exciting to break a door down than to show somebody a warrant and ask to be admitted), the dramatic images can all too easily be interpreted as an argument about real-life crime and real-life police methods.

Dirty Harry is not a simple-minded film, however. While Eastwood was able to argue for Harry in terms of a higher morality and in later films (*Magnum Force* especially) presented him as merely a mechanic making adjustments to a still workable system, Siegel had no such pat message. When Siegel's Harry Callahan throws his badge away at the film's end, he throws away his legitimacy. There is that much doubt in Siegel's mind.

Dirty Harry is set in San Francisco, which is itself interesting. San Francisco, while being a city, is not New York. In the American symbolic landscape the East is identified with civilisation and civilised values, the West is the frontier and, by association, the symbol of frontier ethics, 'non-conformism' and individualism. San Francisco is a western town (much more so than Los Angeles) — in fact, it is the last western town before the great Pacific Ocean, the last frontier. But even San Francisco is 'civilised' and while Walt Coogan could return to the West after his sojourn among the skyscrapers, Harry Callahan's West is all but indistinguishable from the rest of the concrete jungle.

At the beginning of *Dirty Harry* the camera focuses on a sniper picking out his victims from a roof-top vantage point. This is Scorpio (Andy Robinson) hiding out among the 'mountainous terrain' of the urban landscape. He shoots a young girl in a swimming pool and makes off. When Harry Callahan arrives at the scene he discovers a note left by Scorpio announcing that his next target will be "a nigger or a Catholic priest". The killer is indiscriminate but not irrational. Scorpio demands a ransom of $200,000 and kidnaps a fourteen-year old girl, holding her for a hostage. Having killed three times by now, the city's mayor (John Vernon) is prepared to pay the ransom. Harry argues against giving in to Scorpio and says that he is convinced that the girl is already dead. The mayor disagrees and allows Harry to deliver the money, in a half-hearted attempt to capture Scorpio.

Scorpio leads Harry round San Francisco by phoning through a series of messages in a succession of phone booths. Eventually, Scorpio and Harry confront each other in a park. Scorpio beats up Harry, whose partner Chico (Reni Santoni) arrives in time to be seriously wounded by Scorpio. Harry stabs Scorpio before passing out and Scorpio leaps off like a wounded animal into the undergrowth.

Acting against orders Harry gives chase and tracks Scorpio down by finding the doctor who has treated Scorpio's knife wound. He traces him to a room beneath the stands at a football stadium, chases him onto the field, shoots him and tortures him to find out where the girl is. The girl is dead, but Scorpio is released because of Harry's manifestly illegal treatment of him.

Harry is reprimanded, but he is convinced that Scorpio will kill again and follows him. Scorpio pays to have himself beaten up so he can blame Harry, and while Harry is defending himself, Scorpio kidnaps a bus full of school children to hold them for ransom. He demands money and a plane out of the

> **Don Siegel: Clint has an absolute fixation as an anti-hero. It's his credo in life and in all the films he has done so far and it has been very successful — certainly for Clint and for those who own a piece of his pictures**

country. The city authorities and the mayor agree, but Harry decides to try and capture Scorpio. He finds the bus, jumps onto it and forces it off the road. After a brief chase and shoot-out Harry corners Scorpio. Echoing a speech he made earlier in the film when arresting a bank-robber Harry confronts the cowering Scorpio. Earlier he had spoken coolly — this time there is rage in his voice:

"I know what you're thinking punk. You're thinking he has fired six shots or only five. Now to tell you the truth, I forgot myself in this excitement. But being as this is a 44 Magnum, the most powerful handgun in the world, that will blow your head clean off, you gotta ask yourself a question. Do I feel lucky? Well, do you — punk?"

Scorpio giggles nervously and moves towards his gun. This time, unlike before, Harry squeezes the trigger. Having executed his prey Harry walks off and, in recognition of his responsibility, he casts his police badge into the river. He is isolated, alone in the city, and unlike *Coogan's Bluff* the city is everywhere.

There is little doubt that *Dirty Harry* is an anti-liberal film. Harry Callahan's character apart, the combination of certain stock attitudes typical of Siegel with a lack of social or psychological depth directly contradicts some of the most hallowed liberal images. Hippies and blacks are associated with crime and perversion. The film is anti-feminine (though not explicitly anti-woman) and maintains a generally high moral tone about sexual and social deviance, and while it recognises violence as a social *problem* the causes of and solutions to the problem are presented, if at all, through a conventional imagery of villains and heroes.

To some extent, however, Harry and Scorpio are identified — as one would expect of a film built around an elaborate hunt. Scorpio is almost Harry's alter-ego — equally rootless, equally cunning, equally sadistic; a man who demonstrably hates women, blacks, Catholics and the young. But there is one fundamental difference — Scorpio is on the side of evil and Harry is on the side of good, or at least Scorpio is an agent of chaos while Harry is an

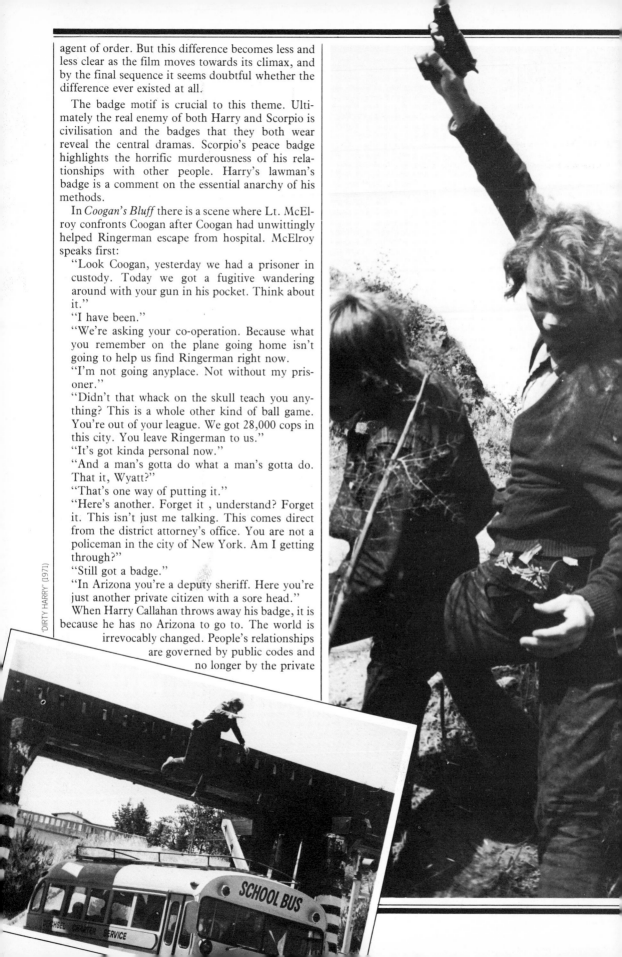

agent of order. But this difference becomes less and less clear as the film moves towards its climax, and by the final sequence it seems doubtful whether the difference ever existed at all.

The badge motif is crucial to this theme. Ultimately the real enemy of both Harry and Scorpio is civilisation and the badges that they both wear reveal the central dramas. Scorpio's peace badge highlights the horrific murderousness of his relationships with other people. Harry's lawman's badge is a comment on the essential anarchy of his methods.

In *Coogan's Bluff* there is a scene where Lt. McElroy confronts Coogan after Coogan had unwittingly helped Ringerman escape from hospital. McElroy speaks first:

"Look Coogan, yesterday we had a prisoner in custody. Today we got a fugitive wandering around with your gun in his pocket. Think about it."

"I have been."

"We're asking your co-operation. Because what you remember on the plane going home isn't going to help us find Ringerman right now.

"I'm not going anyplace. Not without my prisoner."

"Didn't that whack on the skull teach you anything? This is a whole other kind of ball game. You're out of your league. We got 28,000 cops in this city. You leave Ringerman to us."

"It's got kinda personal now."

"And a man's gotta do what a man's gotta do. That it, Wyatt?"

"That's one way of putting it."

"Here's another. Forget it , understand? Forget it. This isn't just me talking. This comes direct from the district attorney's office. You are not a policeman in the city of New York. Am I getting through?"

"Still got a badge."

"In Arizona you're a deputy sheriff. Here you're just another private citizen with a sore head."

When Harry Callahan throws away his badge, it is because he has no Arizona to go to. The world is irrevocably changed. People's relationships are governed by public codes and no longer by the private

'DIRTY HARRY' (1971)

code of the westerner and Harry's action is the final rejection of the public codes. He throws his badge away because a man of his kind no longer has a social role. He is one of a dying breed.

This is Siegel's ending, of course. Eastwood's objections to it stem from his notion of the higher morality that his heroes are always supposed to carry around with them like some mental bible. The ending as it stands affects the whole tone of the film. Siegel's attack on liberalism is from an individualist position verging on nihilism. In Siegel's world the outsider is virtuous partly *because* he is an outsider. Eastwood's outsider is a gallant representative of some greater good. To throw away the badge is for him a rejection of that greater good, a denial of the morality of which the law is an imperfect and changeable image. Of course it's not a fascist position. To call it fascist is to misuse language. More than that, it is to misconstrue the complex realities of the contemporary world. In *Magnum Force* Eastwood (as Harry) replied to the critics of *Dirty Harry* and pointed to his dispute with Siegel over the badge sequence. Confronted by the rogue cop Briggs who wants Harry to join his band of vigilantes, Harry argues against their illegal methods. Briggs speaks first:

"What the hell do you know about the law? You're a great cop, Harry. You've got a chance to join the team but you'd rather stick with the system."

"Briggs, I hate the goddammed system, but until someone comes along with some changes that make sense I'll stick with it."

"You're about to become extinct!"

Trying to keep the system in harness with a higher morality leads to considerable difficulties, and is probably a misguided endeavour in the first place. Where the higher morality comes from is never one of Harry's first questions, but that morality is nonetheless real to Eastwood. And civilisation is an even less avoidable fact, Eastwood's Harry Callahan has to recognise the need for legitimacy and its badges. It's a righteous vision. In groping for a reconciliation between the increasingly corrupt and ineffective system that is legitimised and the higher morality that is supposed, through law, to legitimise it, Eastwood's heros are bound to break·out of the confining shell of conservatism. Sooner or later they must strive for alternatives — so as to avoid becoming extinct.

CHAPTER 4
HOUR OF THE 44 MAGNUM (1971-76)

'THEN THE LAW'S CRAZY'

Actors and directors continually slide up and down the greasy pole of critical acclaim, and it is never hard to find a good number pushing up the standards by which their successor will be praised or condemned. But actors and directors who seem in some weird and wonderful way to define the times for those who live in them are rare, and it is Eastwood's importance in this respect that makes him so interesting. Why and how does the persona he has created strike such a chord in the audience? The answer does not lie in any superlative talents he may possess as an actor or director. Such chords are not struck by talent or vision, though it would be unusual to find behind a persona of this social significance someone with none of either. Eastwood has some of both, but like most top box office stars he is more of an ideal mirror to the times than an outstanding talent in his own right. What makes him so ideal?

Mirrors to the times are notoriously dubious affairs. Nixon mirrored the same times as Eastwood, but then so did Bob Dylan and the Women's Movement. Take television News, which supposedly defines itself as a changing mirror to what is actually happening. It is not a very accurate one. What is reported is often dealt with in highly partisan terms, from Establishment bias in politics down to nationalist bias in sport. More important is the selection of what is reported. Men on strike at a factory are newsworthy, men working at the same factory are not. Fred and Alice falling in love in Bolton is as un-newsworthy as the continual high lead-content in the air we breathe; Prince Charles falling in love is information as vital as the continual lowering of the value of the pounds we spend. The News doesn't tell you what is happening, it tells you what news is happening. A mirror to a mirror, a simple tautology.

Movies though are not generally concerned with shuffling information. The mirrors they hold to the world are many and various. They reflect, they mould, they confirm. Some are supposed to show the life, the partner, the money you wish you had. Some are supposed to show what lies further beneath the surface; personal and social realities are petrified on film for those who are too busy living them to work out what they look like. Increasingly, in the last twenty years films have sought to present both sorts of mirror, to be entertaining and possessed of depth, to be art that makes money. The modern film becomes the meeting ground of the traditional 'star' and the issues of social concern. The personae created by the likes of Eastwood take on a political dimension, whether the star likes it or not.

This is not necessarily a problem. The Leone films had a strong political dimension in the widest sense, but it was never defined nor should have been. It was the very lack of definition that struck such a strong chord in audiences. No Name was in control of his world, a staggering political reality that was not transferable to the suburban deserts of the developed world. Bounty hunting could never recover from the introduction of police computers. No Name was a political metaphor; he demonstrated what civilisation has cost through the medium of a mythic environment. No more, no less.

Dirty Harry also works on the level of escapist entertainment, but it does so amidst an environment that cannot be escaped. Harry Callahan is a bounty hunter who only gets wages, but who has access to the computer. Like No Name he vividly demonstrates a desire for those simple values that civilisation has ploughed under, but since, unlike No Name, he operates in the here and now, he is also living proof of what we have been saddled with instead. In confronting the problems of the contemporary world he is forced, by the nature of his calling, to get his hands 'dirty' in the search for solutions. In his choice of life-style and work-style he lays himself open to criticism by those who would do the job differently. By choosing such a central character both Eastwood and Siegel laid themselves open to attack. The political dimension is too well-defined and central to be ignored.

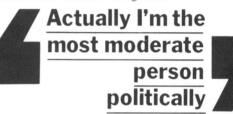

Actually I'm the most moderate person politically

Like the television News *Dirty Harry* is made up of what it says, how it says it, and what it neglects to mention. All three are naturally inter-related, but it is also clear that the political dimension varies from one to the other. The story itself is innocent enough. Scorpio, a mad killer, is hounded to death by Harry Callahan through the maze of illegal corruption (crime) and legal corruption (the city authorities). It is something that could and does happen.

The telling of the story — the delineation of characters and situations — is something else again. Harry himself is no revolutionary socialist, but then very few who are work for the San Francisco Police Department. His methods are rough-and-ready to say the least, but given the nature of his adversary, they seem appropriate. They work. The other characters offer more cause for concern. Scorpio wears a huge peace-symbol buckle on his belt; the legal adviser who advises his release happens to come from Berkeley. These two incidentals could be seen as red rags to rouse the rednecks, asserting by inference that all who wear peace signs are psychopaths and that anyone connected with Berkeley is a liberal schmuck. It would seem more reasonable to see them as Siegel baiting those who think symbols and ideologies more telling than what the people who wear them actually do.

One major criticism of *Dirty Harry* is that it allows both interpretations regardless of Siegel's intentions. Scorpio and the authorities can be seen as liberalism gone berserk, and Harry as the avenging

angel straight out of the old frontier, come to give the pansies a shot or two of moral authority. The film can also be seen as the story of one man bitterly trying to do a job that's damn near impossible, caught as he is between corruption above and below. For Siegel certainly the film states a problem, it does not push solutions. The last scene, in which Harry throws away his badge and his role, implicitly admits that there are none.

Most telling of all are the facts that *Dirty Harry* neglects to mention. Scorpio enjoys killing; it is impossible not to identify with his pursuer. But there are other kinds of criminal, both those who wish to climb out of poverty in the only way left to them, and those who oppose the liberal establishment not from the Right but from the Left. For Siegel these might as well not exist. In *Dirty Harry* there is only corruption and Harry himself, its moralistic nemesis. This conflict justifies Harry's monomaniacal assault on society, but it also makes his isolation inevitable. Like No Name he controls situations with his gun, but beyond those situations is something guns can no longer control. A few deaths no longer turn the trick. The city is bigger than he is, the days of the crusading individualist are gone. *Dirty Harry* acknowledges this. Harry Callahan is as much a victim as everybody else; the film ends with him isolated and futureless. It is a nihilistic film.

If this in itself was acceptable the political implications for the future were less so. If Siegel's Harry — or a similar character in the same sort of set-up — were to be later romanticised by Eastwood then Paulene Kael's charge of fascism could appear far more apt. Romantic nihilism is very close to fascism. The obvious answer was to de-romanticise Harry, to make him more accessible, more vulnerable. But this threatened the very essence of the romantic loner image which has constituted the Eastwood persona.

For the moment he avoided the issue, returning to a time and place where moralistic loners were still effective and didn't get labelled as fascists, down on the border, down Mexico way . . .

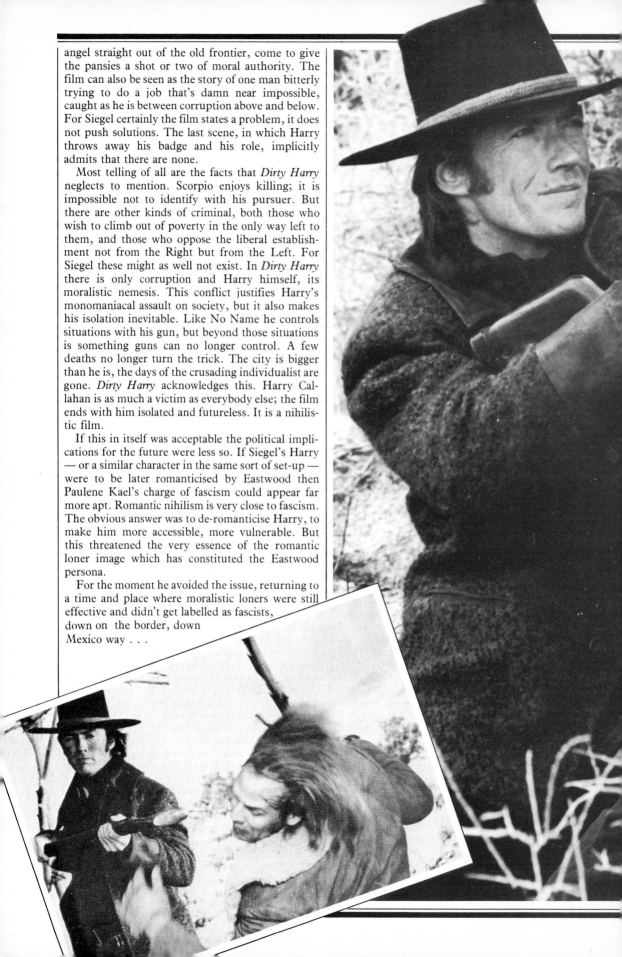

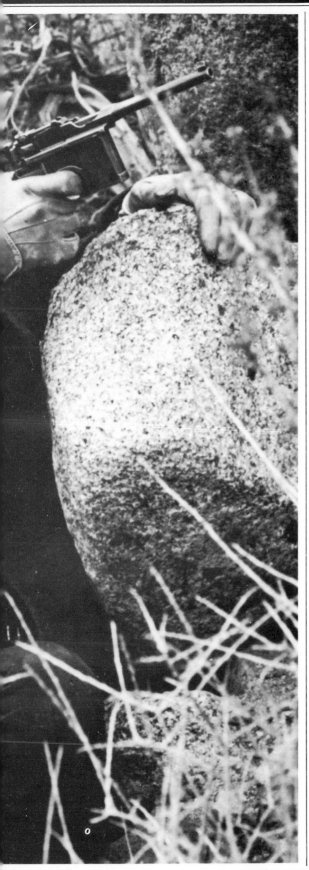

RETURN OF THE LONE STRANGER

The western has always operated on different levels from that of the crime film. The latter traditionally carries a strong documentary streak, the former lies more in the realm of parable. Issues, like the landscape, are larger than life. They can afford to be, for the characters on screen are not characters the audience will meet on the streets or see on the News. This, of course, is what makes the western an escapist genre par excellence. A good story, plenty of action, and a message or theme vague enough to carry emotional power without requiring too much thought.

The message though is no less crucial for being vague. Westerns, at some level, are concerned with the taming and settling of a wilderness by civilised society, and with the transition from the individual's assertion of civilised values to their eventual social enforcement. The romantic loner, half-in and half-out of civilisation is the advance guard of civilisation's spread, which he both romanticises and legitimises. This smooth transition from the freedom of the frontier to the Great Society is at the core of the as-yet-unrealised American Dream. Both Republicans and Democrats have their own ideas as to how it should be achieved, and naturally they each have their own westerns to serve as examples.

Chisum is a classic 'Republican' western, a John Wayne vehicle directed by Andrew McLaglen in 1970. It is a classic case of the western whose primary theme is the introduction of civilised values to the frontier. These values are successfully grafted onto the rough-and-ready frontier spirit in the persona of Wayne's hero. The corrupt civilisation of Europe and the East becomes the pure civilisation of the fenced range. Chisum himself, who would be a nasty capitalist back East becomes a benevolent father-figure in this purer atmosphere. As a moral figure — and a figure who stands for the spread of morality — he has all the usual arrogance and self-righteousness. Here we see the seeds of Vietnam. As Jenni Calder puts it in *There Must Be A Lone Ranger*: "*Chisum* is a corporation western, a western that extols benevolent dictatorship. What gives Chisum the right to be a dictator? The fact that he has fought and suffered for his gains; the fact that he has won. The Mexican peasants have not won. They are still struggling with the soil and the water. And they will never win, because they are inferior, and need the kindly protection of the big man in order to survive. It is a reflection, and the fact that we see it in a western makes it a wistful reflection, of the role many Americans would like to see their country playing in the world."

Chisum wants to have his cake and eat it, to be both frontier hero and patron of the arts; the gunfighter heroes of a 'Democrat' western like *The Magnificent Seven* are not so greedy. They too help the Mexican peasants, but as brother-figures rather than benevolent dictators. There is none of the contempt for 'inferior beings' that characterises *Chisum*.

'JOE KIDD' (1972) INSET: WITH DON STROUD

It is in fact the Mexican peasants who win, even though they are still struggling with the soil and the water. They admire the gunfighters for their power and freedom, they use them to safeguard their lives, but they can offer them no permanent place, no respite from the emptiness of power and freedom without responsibilities or companionship. The gunfighters are a vanishing breed and they know it. Their heroism is tragic, their decision to help the peasants a conscious martyrdom. This too is a reflection of the role many Americans would like to see their country playing in the world. These are the Americans who thought that helping the Vietnamese was a duty not to be shirked, who were monstrously naive rather than merely arrogant.

Both these approaches are moralistic, and the crucial fact about moralistic heroes is their inability to control their environment by any means other than domination. They either succeed like Chisum and establish a quasi-fascist empire, or recognise their limitations like Brynner and McQueen in *The Magnificent Seven*. Or Harry Callahan. If Brynner had had a badge he'd have thrown it away at the end of the film. Only the amoral hero — No Name — has

none of that need to impress his values on all and sundry. Only he can come back again and again without destroying his credibility.

Joe Kidd (1972) attempts to synthesise the 'Democrat' western with the Leone western. Sturges was the director (he had also directed *The Magnificent Seven*) who attempted to give No Name morality without destroying his romantic loner image. The result was confusion. As one critic put it: "in his single-minded purpose of turning the corrupt Mexican over to a corrupt justice he (Joe Kidd) is demonstrably mad".

> In retrospect I think there's a certain escapism . . . to a less complicated era, more a do-it-yourself era, so to speak

The plot and character seem more akin to *Dirty Harry* than to Leone's westerns. Joe Kidd joins a posse of hired guns recruited by a big landowner to track down a Mexican bandit-chief who has been terrorising the neighbourhood in traditional style. Joe eventually comes to realise that the issues are not as simple as they seem, and that the big landowner has been terrorising the local Mexican peasants with no less vigour. Good becomes bad so bad becomes good. He changes sides, wins the range-war for the Mexicans, and then discovers that the bandit-chief is no Robin Hood figure. Bad stays bad and good becomes bad. Everyone is bad. At this point he has reached the awareness of universal corruption that No Name always took for granted. But still he persists, defeating the landowner and taking in the bandit-chief. Hence the above conclusion that he is demonstrably mad, since any sane individual would turn their backs on the whole sordid mess. Joe, instead, does a Dirty Harry. He winds up the entire operation and then presumably throws away his badge.

More depressing, Joe Kidd's high moral purpose is supported by the traditional American virtues of strength and determination. The wit and intelligence of No Name have all but disappeared beneath a blanket self-righteousness. Even driving a train through a saloon wall in moving homage to Magritte is no substitute for a piece of No Name's effortless ingenuity. Joe Kidd is never in control of anything but his gun. There is nothing distinctive about him.

Which could not be said of the stranger in *High Plains Drifter* (1972), the second film directed by Eastwood himself. Here we have No Name being amoral in the name of morality. Another twist in the screw.

The opening shot is beautiful. From out of a slow-dancing heat-haze a lone horseman rides towards the audience, gradually acquiring definition. Because of the mirage-effect, and because a telephoto lens is used, the horseman seems to be gliding through the sky. When he reaches the town of Lago the townsfolk, each face examined at length, stare at him with what could be recognition, could be merely apprehension. The significance of all these images will be explained as the film unfolds.

For the moment the stranger is not bursting to explain himself. "What did you say your name was?" asks the chatty town dwarf. "I didn't" the stranger mutters as he stares into the distance. He's only there for a drink and a bath, or so it seems. Still, just in case, the three men hired by the town to discourage strangers are sent to discourage him. They die, and from this point on the stranger reigns as virtual dictator of Lago. This political arrangement is not, as it turns out, inimical to the townsfolk, since they are expecting a visit from three gunmen — predecessors of the stranger's victims — with a debt of vengeance to settle. The town needs protection, and this deadly stranger is the only obvious candidate for the task.

The stranger, after initial hesitation, agrees to train the townsmen in the noble art of self-defence provided that they do whatever he asks and furnish

his every requirement. They agree to this, but the stranger's wants prove to be extremely bizarre. He immediately appoints the dwarf both mayor and sheriff, and starts stripping the town of its property in aid of a picnic. He sequesters food, drink, bed-sheets, and has a barn pulled down to provide wood for picnic-tables. He does indeed start to train the men in self-defence, but neglects to provide the women with any against himself. He decides to live alone in the hotel, so all the other guests have to be ejected. Everyone is paying, but exactly what for is not made clear. Finally he has the whole town painted blood-red and changes its name from Lago to Hell.

While all this is happening there are periodic flashbacks of the town's previous Marshal, Jim Duncan, being whipped to death in the mainstreet by the three men who have just been released from jail and whom the town is now expecting. The Marshal himself, shot from a difficult angle, looks uncannily like the stranger. We later learn that the Marshal had discovered that the mine, the town's economic *raison d'etre*, was on Government land and hence illegal. For insisting on reporting this fact he had been murdered by the three gunmen with the town's acquiescence. The gunmen had been sent to jail, but the town's guilt has not been punished. Though insisting that his death was 'the price of progress' their part in it is not something they wish to be reminded of. His grave, though marked, has not been named. And a man lying in an unnamed

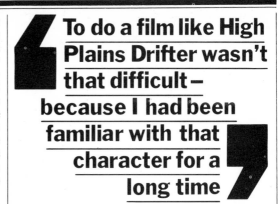

grave, as the stranger philosophically confides in the dwarf, is unable to rest easy.

In the meantime the three killers are getting nearer, callously murdering some men for their horses. The stranger has the bedsheets converted into a 'Welcome Home Boys' sign which is hung above the street. By this time the townsfolk have become so incensed by the stranger's mocking manner that the approaching killers seem a merely secondary threat. A number of them resolve to kill the stranger, but naturally he is one step ahead of them, casually tossing a stick of dynamite into the room where they are busily beating a dummy to death in his bed. Several die in the resultant chaos, and next morning the killers at last loom on the horizon. The stranger leaves the town to save itself by its own

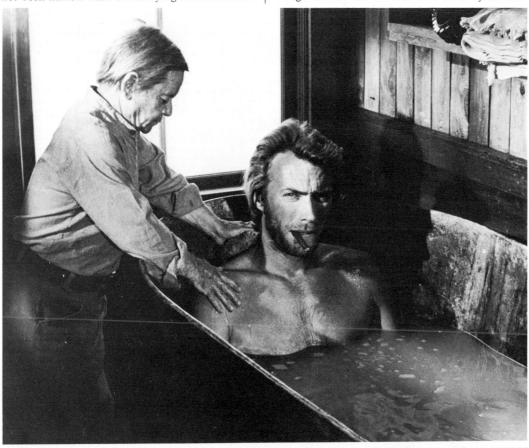

efforts, in which task they prove lamentably inadequate. The gunmen spend the day killing whom they feel like killing, and by nightfall have herded the rest into the saloon for the traditional gloat. By this time half the town is on fire, looking even more like its new name. Vengeance is nigh. A bullwhip snakes out of the darkness and drags a killer into the street. He dies. Another is hung with the whip, the third — the leader — is shot dead whimpering "who are you?", his face a case-study in supernatural dread.

This question is repeated by the dwarf as the stranger passes him on his way out of town. The dwarf is naming the dead Marshal's grave. "You know who I am", says the stranger, and goes out the way he comes in, gliding slowly away through the whirl of mirages into the distance. He can rest easy now. The haze is his de-incarnation.

High Plains Drifter, though a strange film, is not a very complex one. It looks superficially like an Eastwood imitation of Leone. As the *Financial Times* reviewer noted: "The Leone trademarks are all well in evidence: the long, brooding pauses, the low angle camera shots, the percussive score, the satirical treatment of the town's corrupt hierarchy." The hero has no name, he is all-powerful, he wields it amorally. But these similarities in style and characterisation are only that. This No Name has a name, albeit one the world is trying to forget. In the Leone films the mystery of his character wanders ever-unexplained through the plot; in *High Plains Drifter* the mystery *is* the plot. And most important, this No Name's amoral behaviour is sanctioned by others' immoral behaviour. He can do whatever he wants because he has been wronged before the film even begins. As in *Dirty Harry* the deck is stacked. The situation has been created to legitimise the hero.

Of course, as the film is a western, the deck has been stacked in a very different manner. The stranger has none of Harry's irksome limitations. He *is* bigger than the town in which he seeks justice. This individual *can* act as social judge, jury and executioner. And as if that wasn't enough he himself is as invulnerable as only a ghost can be. In this light Eastwood's comment on the film — "it didn't have to be a western, it was just a small morality play . . . it was just a vignette of a certain attitude" — takes on an ominous ring. As a statement of concern regarding people's reluctance to involve themselves in situations demanding moral involvement, the message of the morality play is transferable from Lago to contemporary America. But as a statement of solution it is not. All-powerful ghosts full of Old Testament fervour are no answer to the social diseases of contemporary America, no matter how stylish their *modus operandi*.

Having said all that it is possible to express admiration for Eastwood's execution of the film. Despite some erratic editing it looks very good, a quality due in no small measure to the natural beauty of the Mono Lake location. In Eastwood's words: "We selected a highly photogenic area for the location . . . the brilliant colours of the backgrounds and the

> 'I suppose my involvement goes even deeper than acting or directing. I love every aspect of the creation of motion pictures and I guess I am committed to it for life'

constantly changing cloud formations gave us the opportunity to get some very effective shots." The camera-work is as stylish as the hero; the story is well-told, integrating dramatic action with touches of surrealistic wit. Eastwood was clearly becoming a more-than-competent director.

But he was no closer to solving — or realising — the basic dilemma in his persona raised by *Dirty Harry*. The stranger in *High Plains Drifter*, when all is said and done, is an attractive character but not an admirable one. Which raises questions about the method of attraction. Power and style are usually attractive, but are only acceptable when the person possessing them in turn accepts the limitations of his environment. This is what No Name does. They are still attractive, but not acceptable, when a moral monomaniac seeks to dominate a community with them. Yet both *Dirty Harry* and *High Plains Drifter* are built round such a hero. In both cases it seems justifiable — this is the way the films are set up — but in neither case is it made clear that these are exceptional circumstances. One is left with the chilling impression that such a hero is intended to be universally applicable.

'HIGH PLAINS DRIFTER' (1972)

A MISTAKE OR THREE

For all the doubts that the political implications of Clint Eastwood's later heroes have raised in any critical breast to the left of centre, it cannot be denied that the man has made a number of films of compelling power. The two of course are connected. *Dirty Harry* and *High Plains Drifter* are both intensely watchable and interesting films; they touch on attitudes and situations whose controversial character is bound to stimulate debate and criticism. You can't make an omelette without breaking eggs, as they say. Eastwood, while still some way from an omelette to please the liberal palate, has certainly broken a number of cinematic eggs.

But with the completion of *High Plains Drifter* he seemed to enter a period of partially suspended animation. With the exception of *Magnum Force* (the second Harry Callahan film, which is discussed in the following section) the films he made in the period 1973-5 were singularly uninspiring, highly derivative and completely uncontroversial. The first of these, *Breezy*, was the first film he directed but did not star in.

Breezy (1973) is the story of a seventeen-year-old girl's relationship with a fifty-year-old real estate dealer. He is a conventional character, bitter about his recent divorce but still clinging to the social niceties. One day he sees this scruffy-looking young lady hitching outside his house and gives her a lift to town, less out of human kindness than from a desire to re-establish the tone of the neighbourhood. She chats away, they find a wounded dog and, after hesitation on his part, come to its rescue. That seems to be that, but the next day the police arrive with Breezy at his house. She has claimed to be his niece. He goes along with the deception and soon they are in bed together. As the relationship develops and the dog recovers he begins to experience doubts. His friends all tell him she is young enough to be his grand-daughter etc, and her friends he finds completely alien to anything he has ever known. He eventually tells her the relationship is over, but soon after this a friend's husband is killed in a road accident and he is brought by proxy to an acknowledgement of his own loneliness. He and Breezy start again and live(?) ever after.

Like *Play Misty For Me*, *Breezy* centres on a relationship haunted by conflict. William Holden as the real estate dealer and Kate Lenz as Breezy are both impressive, and the relationship is well-observed, if lacking the psycho-dramatics that characterised *Play Misty For Me*. But as in the previous film the relationship seems to exist in a vacuum, for the social environment is completely unconvincing. His friends are a cross between real people and clichés from the Great American Middle-Aged Neurosis syndrome, hers are just clichés. One suspects that Eastwood has little understanding of, or sympathy for, that large part of American youth which has been characterised as an 'alternative culture'. In all his modern-day films youth has received something of a raw deal. In *Coogan's Bluff* it was portrayed as addled by drugs and short on backbone; in *Dirty*

'I don't know enough, I'll never learn everything I need to learn. When a guy thinks he's already learned it he can only go backwards'

Harry and *The Enforcer* it was the prime enemy of Eastwood's avenging policeman. Only in *Thunderbolt And Lightfoot* and *The Outlaw Josey Wales* has a younger man shared the glory, in both cases as a disciple of Eastwood's character, and in both cases ending up dead. Yet in *Breezy* youth culture is supposedly half the background. Its portrayal as the unrecognisable clichés that Eastwood and his scriptwriters take to be 'hippies' is appalling. By 1973 someone should have known better.

This failure to provide the central relationship with a social context of any conviction makes *Breezy* little more than a well-acted soap opera. One reviewer pulled out the ultimate insult: it was "more like a television feature". The *Variety* reviewer was more explicit: Eastwood was "failing on the side of restraint (to put it gently) or else inarticulated shallowness of character development and emotional expression (to lay it out plainly)."

This criticism could be applied with equal conviction to Eastwood's next-but-one acting role. *Thunderbolt And Lightfoot* was written and directed by Michael Cimino, with Eastwood and Jeff Bridges in the title roles. They are a pair of loners, one a bankrobber, the other a young outcast, who share the search for a living in the outlands of contemporary America. The story is set amidst the mountains of Idaho and Montana, and the continual interweaving of driving sequences and shots of scenic grandeur are not the only echoes of *Easy Rider*. Here too we have two basically likeable characters — younger optimist, older sceptic — who drive blithely on, having a good time, until the inevitable tragedy catches up with them.

There is no doubt that Lightfoot is the more interesting character. Eastwood's best scenes are at the beginning, in particular the sight of him preaching from a pulpit, all slicked-back hair and spectacles. But then an old bank-robbing partner catches up with him and, after an exhausting run across a cornfield, he is picked up by Lightfoot. As their relationship develops the fun is left to the younger man, with the older taking on a father-figure role and only coming to life in the display of his professional expertise.

The plot centres around two robberies of the Montana Armoury vaults. The first occurs before the film begins. Thunderbolt had taken part in it and, in the ensuing hue and cry, hidden the money. His confederates think he has double-crossed them, and they catch up with him and Lightfoot outside the school where the money was hidden. Unfortunately the school has been replaced by a modern school; progress has overtaken them, literally as well as metaphorically. Thunderbolt manages to convince (somewhat unconvincingly) his ex-partners of his faithfulness, and Lightfoot suggests that they do the robbery again. The idea is greeted with hoots of derisive laughter and then accepted. What else is there to do?

The planning goes ahead with Lightfoot's youthful insolence getting heavily on one of the partner's nerves. They successfully accomplish the robbery, but find themselves cornered in a drive-in movie park. Another car-chase ensues (about the fourth), in which one of the partners gets killed and the other goes berserk, knocking out Thunderbolt and kicking in the side of Lightfoot's head, before driving

> **I try to approach film emotionally – how it moves me . . . I can intellectualise . . . but if you start out on an intellectual level, I think you're starting without the nucleus**

back into town. There he crashes his car through a store window and has his throat torn out by a guard-dog straight out of *The Hound Of The Baskervilles*. Meanwhile Thunderbolt and Lightfoot are hitching their way to safety, the youngster in none-too-steady a condition, when they stumble upon the old schoolhouse which has been re-erected in the middle of nowhere as an historic monument. They retrieve the money and head for the hills. Lightfoot, with a crashing echo of *Easy Rider*, insists that "we made it" before dying.

The fact that his death is no emotional shock to anyone in the audience is indicative of the film's lightweight style. The jokey relationship between the two heroes is extremely enjoyable, but it is the *only* relationship they seem to have. Similarly the surface of contemporary America is played with a nice irony. People have so many credit cards they look like packs of playing cards; girls on motorbikes carry baseball bats for hitting cars carrying men who try to introduce themselves. One man who picks up Thunderbolt and Lightfoot drives his car drunkenly on and off the road, stops, lets about fifty white rabbits out of his trunk, and proceeds to shoot them with a shotgun. These are all lovely touches, and only lovely touches. The film never transcends its parts; there is no real power in its portrayal of either characters or the world in which they move.

Thunderbolt And Lightfoot is no "right wing Easy Rider" either, as one critic suggested. Its heroes in

WITH JEFF BRIDGES (WEARING WIG) IN 'THUNDERBOLT AND LIGHTFOOT' (1974)

fact are neither as self-consciously heroic as Fonda and Hopper in the original, nor as romanticised as the heroes of the other obvious parallel, *Bonnie And Clyde*. Thunderbolt and Lightfoot are both quite realistic characters, which perhaps expains why Jeff Bridges made such a great success out of his role while Eastwood, more used to playing larger-than-life characters, is as anonymous as he's been since *Where Eagles Dare*.

Another film with no real power in its portrayal of either its characters or the world in which it moves, but also lacking in lovely touches or any sense of fun, is *The Eiger Sanction*. The great mystery about this film is why it was made at all. Eastwood himself, interviewed in 1976, seemed none too sure. "I took a book Universal owned and I couldn't figure out what to do", he says. The book in question was a best-seller for reasons best-known to that public who bought it. The central character is Jonathan Hemlock, an art lecturer who carries out assassinations for a hopefully fictitious American Intelligence

 Brian Hutton: Regardless if he's good or bad, at least he's certain

Agency as the means to get enough money for improving his illicit collection of paintings. The plot has him blackmailed by the Intelligence Agency into carrying out an assassination (a 'sanction') whilst climbing the North Face of the Eiger. Throughout the book and film the 'hero' stays as cold as the mountain he intends to climb, and far less interesting.

Eastwood: "It didn't have the kind of a story you could tell with *Play Misty's* kind of impact and excitement. The only excitement you could do was on a visual level and that is the way it was written. I would have liked, in a way, to have done *The Eiger Sanction* as a not-so-satiric, maybe serious adventure story . . ."

But he didn't. Rather, as Richard Combs wrote in *Monthly Film Bulletin*: "tucked snugly into the lining of every crisp mouthful of dialogue is a well-known wisecrack. All the villains have been constructed from pre-fabricated Bond models . . . Most depressing, Eastwood directs in a bland, blunt and boorish fashion, alternating panoramic views of the landscape and equally broad tributes to his macho presence. Where *Play 'Misty' For Me* and *High Plains Drifter* suggested he was capable of bringing a degree of irony to his own image, here Eastwood the director asks of Eastwood the actor only the faint curling of the lip as every female character topples before him, and the more energetic clenching of the teeth through which he can promise 'something massive' for the film's regular bursts of retaliatory violence."

This extremely denigrating review is not far

EASTWOOD is the man..Eiger is the location... and the sanction-is a license to kill!

CLINT EASTWOOD
"THE EIGER SANCTION" AA
GEORGE KENNEDY

co-starring VONETTA McGEE • JACK CASSIDY
A MALPASO COMPANY FILM

From the Suspenseful International-Best-Seller!

'THE EIGER SANCTION' (1975)

wrong. If Eastwood's persona is something of a Jekyll and Hyde affair, then Trevanian's Jonathan Hemlock is tailor-made for Hyde. A cold killer who knows no guilt, a man so scared of women he has to humiliate them. The one consolation to be had from *The Eiger Sanction* is the deep chasm separating any notion of the real world from its glossy-thriller characters and plot. There is none of that dangerous political ambivalence which characterises the Eastwood persona face-to-face with supposed social reality. Hyde has never been as threatening as Jekyll and Hyde.

' It's tough directing myself '

CLINT WITH GEORGE KENNEDY 'THE EIGER SANCTION' (1975)

THE PRICE OF STYLE

During and after this series of undemanding films, in 1973 and 1976, Eastwood returned to the streets of San Francisco to make two more Harry Callahan films, *Magnum Force* and *The Enforcer*. Why did he resurrect the policeman Siegel had confined to a nihilistic oblivion? *Dirty Harry's* huge commercial success is one obvious reason, but there are also others that seem appropriate. *The Enforcer* virtually re-treads the same ground as *Dirty Harry*, indicating a continuing pre-occupation with the character and a belief in the vitality of the issues he raises. *Magnum Force* was clearly intended, and structured, as a direct reply to the original film's critics.

Harry's enemies in *Magnum Force* are a group of young traffic (!) policemen who act out that vigilante version of law enforcement which the critics of *Dirty*

> **The only time I've ever been associated with anything political is by innuendo or by people's assumption that I have certain political aspects**

Harry attributed to Harry himself. Tired of the 'liberal' establishment's benevolent attitude to criminals they start knocking them off (the criminals, that is). Harry, invited to join them, admits that he hates the system, but like Jed Cooper in *Hang 'Em High* (both films were directed by Ted Post) believes the vigilante alternative to be ultimately more disastrous. "When the police start becoming their own executioners, where's it gonna end, huh, Briggs?" he asks the corrupt Lieutenant; "pretty soon you start executin' people for jaywalking, and executin' people for traffic violations, and then you end up executin' your neighbour 'cos his dog pisses on your lawn." At one point Harry feelingly mutters, apparently to Briggs but by implication to his critics: "I'm afraid you've misjudged me."

Paulene Kael still didn't think so. *Magnum Force* was Eastwood's goriest film to date, and the fact that his enemies this time round were Nazi stormtroopers on loan to the S.F.P.D. didn't make Harry's own methods any less satisfactory to the liberal critics. Though his character has been slightly 'softened' — he relates to women (well, sleeps with them), makes more jokes, even seems to have friends — the overwhelming impression is still that of a killing machine fuelled by a huge but unfocused rage.

'MAGNUM FORCE' (1973)

The problem with *Magnum Force* is that, despite its avowed intentions, it cannot disarm Harry's critics without disarming Harry. This is not altogether Eastwood's fault, for the problem lies partly in the very nature of popular entertainment. The 'spectacle' of *Magnum Force* — the plethora of violent deaths which link the story together — is itself offensive, no matter how admirable the theme. In *Magnum Force* the two become fatally intertwined; the spectacle becomes part of the theme, and the theme becomes part of the spectacle.

But at the same time the theme is realistic, the danger not to be discounted, and Harry's methods of overcoming it are effective. It could be said that the offensive nature of the film aptly portrays the offensive nature of the society it mirrors. Paulene Kael thinks Harry "the hero of a totally nihilistic dream world", but though the world is painted like that, Harry's hero-status is far more ambiguous.

> **The idea of purposely setting out to change your image is a futile effort on the part of most actors who have become stars on the basis of what they do best**

Certainly he is stylish and effective wielding his giant phallic 44 Magnum, but little attempt is made to affirm him as a human being. He is not painted as a happy man, as a man who can understand or cope with living. He is a policeman struggling to pull together the letter and the spirit of the Law.

Just how complex the problem of law enforcement has become in recent years was well illustrated by an article in *Village Voice* in Autumn 1973. The police, it stated, "are being asked to do a job which their fellow citizens don't want to do, and which they don't even want to *watch* being done. The police are being asked to function more and more like sanitation workers, taking care of our garbage in a way which neither involves us nor offends our sensibilities. Clean up the scum in Washington Square, but be nice about it. Clear the gay sado hustlers off West Street, but respect sexual preferences. Get the muggers and burglars off my block, but don't violate recent court rulings about loitering rules . . . The limits of acceptable behaviour now border directly on the criminal. This change has worked in favour of virtually every minority and special interest group in the country, whose rights have been expanded and secured. It has also worked in favour of criminals, whose intentions are not equality but felony."

A scene early in *The Enforcer* neatly dramatises this problem. Harry is called to a liquor store where several young maniacs are threatening hostages and demanding a car. Harry decides to give them one, literally, by driving a police car through the storefront. He saves the hostages, and in the process puts three of the hoodlums in hospital. His chief is far from pleased, however. Harry has caused $14,000 worth of damages and the three in hospital are likely to sue for 'excessive use of force'. "For your information", the Captain tells Harry, "the minority community of this city has just about had it with this kind of police work. It's downright disgraceful." To which Harry sarcastically replies: "By minority community I take it you mean the hoods?" Sarcasm is lost on the Captain. "It so happens they're American citizens, too. They happen to have rights." Harry is no more impressed than he was in *Dirty Harry*: "So does that old lady who had a sawed-off shotgun in her ear. Or doesn't she count anymore? What the hell is going on around here? What kind of department are we running when we're more concerned with the rights of the criminals than of the people we're supposed to be protecting?"

On the one hand we have the style and effectiveness of Harry's methods — once again theme and

 I always liked Cagney's style and energy. He was fearless

spectacle mixed together for maximum effect — and on the other hand a distinct feeling that people, on principle, should have precisely those rights which make effective action in this sort of situation ten times as difficult. What is the way out of this dilemma? How would you deal with such a situation? The problem is a real one. Harry, to Eastwood, is trapped in a maze of Catch-22s. He can't enforce the law without breaking it. Whatever he does is wrong.

In *The Enforcer*, as in *Dirty Harry*, the object of Harry's pursuit/vendetta is an unredeemable individual. Bobby Maxwell, like Angel Eyes in *The Good, The Bad And The Ugly*, enjoys killing and shows it. If it is hinted that service in Vietnam has brought him to this inhuman state of mind, it is never suggested that anything but death will cure him. The fact that he kills both Harry's partners only adds more emotional weight to the impossibility of empathising with his plight. In this rigid polarisation of issues *The Enforcer* is as contrived and as open to criticism as *Dirty Harry*.

Neither is this the only example of particular situations being transformed, by sleight of hand, into general statements. At one point Harry is dragged into a restaurant by its owner. A customer has had a heart attack. Harry looks at the stricken individual and . . . kicks him, violently drags him to his feet and out onto the sidewalk, through the outraged clientele. You can almost hear the whispers of 'police brutality'. As it turns out the individual habitually fakes heart-attacks to avoid paying for his

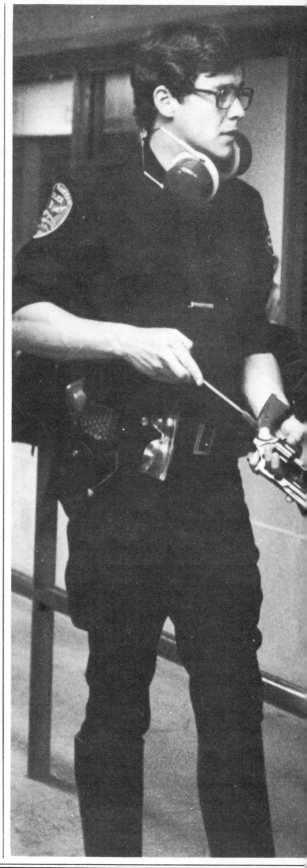

meals. The moral of this little incident: the police are often right when they seem to be wrong. And this of course is a short step from assuming that anything the police do is justified for reasons unknown to the public.

One continuing pre-occupation of the film, which again echoes Siegel's progenitor, is a profound distrust of labels, and particularly new and trendy ones. Bobby Maxwell's group of nutters style themselves The People's Revolutionary Strike Force, but Harry, unlike his superiors, is not about to be taken in by this bullshit. They're after money and thrills, nothing else.

This could be seen as a wholesale smear on liberal/revolutionary ideals, but the treatment of other issues in the film makes it more likely that Eastwood

proportion of women for the high-risk department. Harry is not impressed by the lady's qualifications, reckoning that her inexperience poses a risk to any future partner. It is, he says, a "hell of a price to pay for being stylish".

Naturally, once his old partner has been killed by Bobby, Harry gets Kate as his new one. "Oh shit" is his immediate response. At least his attitude is based on conviction; the Mayor's espousal of her rests purely on a desire for votes, regardless of the consequences which may befall Kate or her co-workers. And if Harry seems justified by Kate's initial bungling, her emergence as a good officer and partner — including saving the old sexist's life — puts him firmly in his place. *The Enforcer* is no advert for traditional sex roles.

The ties Harry has with Kate and his old partner stand in vivid contrast to the corruptness all around. They also make him a more attractive, more vulnerable figure than in the previous films. But even more significant is his relationship with Mohamid, the

> **'A very self-sufficient human being is almost becoming a mythical character in our day and age'**

leader of a non-violent black militant group. Harry goes to Mohamid seeking information and they do a trade — Mohamid'll nose around if Harry puts in a good word for one of his boys on a drugs charge. Mohamid also tells Harry that he's on the wrong side. "You're out there on the street putting your ass on the line for a whole lot of dudes who wouldn't let you in their front door, any more than they would me. As far as they're concerned, you're just another pig, and they hate you for it." "I'm not doing it for them", Harry replies, but when asked who he is doing it for can only say: "you wouldn't believe me if I told you."

Here, for the one and only time in all the Dirty Harry films, Harry comes face to face with someone else who actually believes in something. And though their positions are a world apart, the two feel a certain mutual respect for each other. It is a great shame that Harry never has to confront an enemy like Mohamid, one who would raise more profound questions about his own character and purpose, rather than the infinitely easier targets of corrupt and phoney officialdom and San Francisco's psychotic fringe. Perhaps the forthcoming *Gauntlet*, in which Eastwood again wears a police badge, will see a step or two in this direction. Perhaps not. Either way it is hard not to regret the fundamental weakness expressed in the need to set up each of the Dirty Harry films to make it easy for Harry. The resulting political ambivalence seems a "hell of a price to pay for being stylish".

is saying: people should be judged on what they do, not on what they say or on how they present themselves.

Early in the film Harry, as a punishment for his storefront odyssey, is assigned to Personnel. There he finds himself on a panel interviewing a female officer who is applying to join Homicide. Apparently the Mayor, eager to catch the liberal vote in the forthcoming election, has decreed an increased

CHAPTER 5
'IT SHALL BE LIFE'

A COMMUNE IN TEXAS, 1866 STYLE

It is 1858 in Missouri, close to the Kansas border. The simmering conflict over slavery (or states' rights, depending on your point of view) is coming to the national boil, and nowhere with more bitterness than on this border. Both Kansas and Missouri are divided down the middle, with Kansas leaning to the North, Missouri to the South. On both sides vigilante forces have been formed which conduct raids across the border in an escalating series of reprisals and counter-reprisals.

The Outlaw Josey Wales begins with a scene of dappled yellows, greens and browns. The farmer Josey Wales is ploughing a clearing, helped by his young son. Mum appears downstream, calling the little boy in. Dad is not wearing a gun. This scene, as any student of Leone would know, reeks of vulnerability. What stands between this idyll and the violence of the frontier?

Nothing. Josey looks up a few moments later and sees smoke rising above the trees. He rushes to the house, finds it in flames and surrounded by jeering soldiers wearing red boots — the uniform of the Kansas Red-legs vigilante force. He tries to intervene but is knocked unconscious by a sword. When he comes round his wife and child are dead, his home and life burned to the ground. Later, when Missouri guerrillas pass by on the trail of the Red-legs, he joins them, and for the next seven years, through 'peace' and war, fights for the Confederate cause and acquires a formidable reputation as one of the 'Missouri pistoleers'.

The credits roll across scenes of the Civil War shot in a cold blue light; as they end the band of guerrillas are deciding to give themselves up. The war is over, it is time to go home. Except for Josey — he has no home to go to. His search for one — first in the negative sense of a sanctuary, second in the positive sense of a place to live — is the theme of the film. It will end in another dappled clearing by another stream, with a different woman. Like *High*

Plains Drifter the film turns a full circle. But whereas the earlier film went from death to death through a period of 'life', *The Outlaw Josey Wales* goes from life to life through a period of 'death'.

Josey travels South with Jamie, who alone has survived the Leone-esque massacre of the band by the Union troops they surrendered to. Jamie is badly wounded and Josey helps him; in return Jamie saves Josey from a couple of backwoodsmen eager for bounty money. But soon the younger man dies and Josey has to continue alone. Reaching the relative safety of the Indian Nations he meets Lone Watie,

'THE OUTLAW JOSEY WALES' (1976)

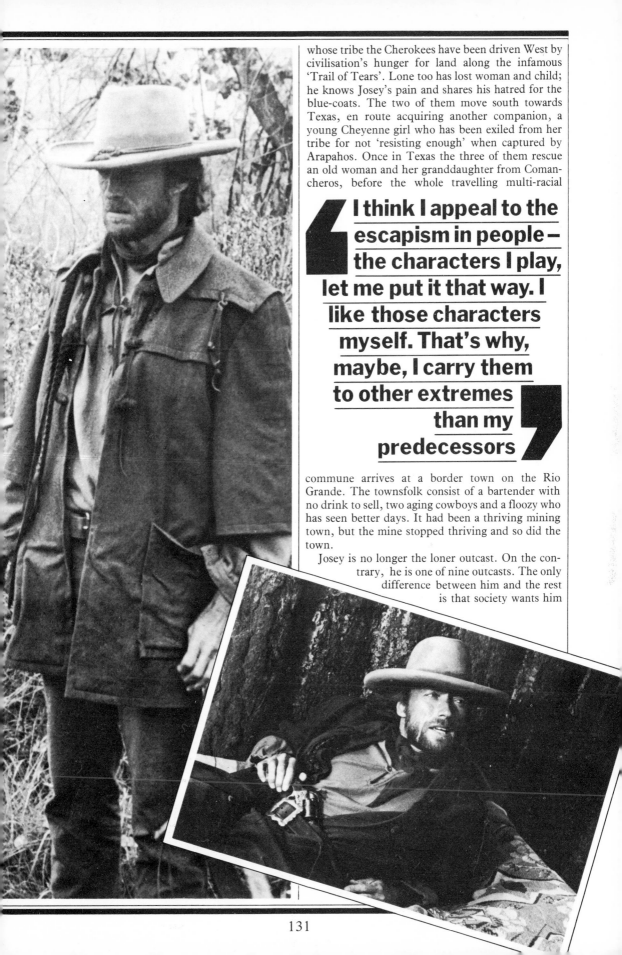

whose tribe the Cherokees have been driven West by civilisation's hunger for land along the infamous 'Trail of Tears'. Lone too has lost woman and child; he knows Josey's pain and shares his hatred for the blue-coats. The two of them move south towards Texas, en route acquiring another companion, a young Cheyenne girl who has been exiled from her tribe for not 'resisting enough' when captured by Arapahos. Once in Texas the three of them rescue an old woman and her granddaughter from Comancheros, before the whole travelling multi-racial

> **I think I appeal to the escapism in people – the characters I play, let me put it that way. I like those characters myself. That's why, maybe, I carry them to other extremes than my predecessors**

commune arrives at a border town on the Rio Grande. The townsfolk consist of a bartender with no drink to sell, two aging cowboys and a floozy who has seen better days. It had been a thriving mining town, but the mine stopped thriving and so did the town.

Josey is no longer the loner outcast. On the contrary, he is one of nine outcasts. The only difference between him and the rest is that society wants him

back — for trial and execution. And while he is waiting for the pursuit to catch up with him, the group as a whole starts to re-create that solidarity among human beings that the society has torn from them. They settle on the old woman's son's farm (he has been killed in the war) and try to start anew. Josey 'negotiates' a deal with the local Comanche chief Ten Bears, and the group as a whole fight off Josey's pursuers. The past can now be forgotten, a fact heavily symbolised by Josey's deepening interest in the granddaughter. The loner has returned home.

'IT'S THE LIVING THAT'S HARD'

Fast and usually violent action sequences traditionally provide much of the 'entertainment' in westerns and crime films. Eastwood's output over the years

has been particularly strong in this respect; it is not hard to remember any number of beautifully choreographed and wittily conceived confrontations between his own lethal persona and a variety of adversaries. *The Outlaw Josey Wales* is no exception. There is one scene set in the trading post where Josey is caught by two bounty-seekers. In handing over his guns he performs the 'border roll', reversing the guns as if by magic to shoot down his captors. This scene is simply exciting; another in which

he appears out of the sun to confront the Comancheros is more. The fight that ensues is dramatic enough, a swirling dance of violence, but the initial appearance itself possesses an almost mystic quality. Here is a man as god, or at the least an archangel. This dimension to the persona is not new; the scene itself echoes No Name's appearance out of the drifting smoke to face Ramon in *A Fistful Of Dollars*.

Such moments are ready-made for Eastwood, the man who looks most impressive moving slowly if at

CLINT EASTWOOD
THE OUTLAW JOSEY WALES

...an army of one.

all, saying little if anything. The man has enormous 'presence', a fact which makes the evocation of such high drama mere child's play. He could doubtless continue to make entertaining films on the strength of this and nothing else. But there are others with great presence — Steve McQueen, for one — who do not make memorable films, who do not challenge the conventions as Eastwood has done with the No Name and Dirty Harry trilogies. An Eastwood film that is merely entertaining — like *Thunderbolt And Lightfoot* or *Hang 'Em High* — is at some level a failure. The persona is more relevant than that. So an extraordinary importance attaches to his choice of material.

The Rebel Outlaw, Josey Wales was written by a 46 year-old half-Cherokee Indian, Forrest Carter. It was the first book he had written, and then only at the insistence of friends who thought that his skill as an oral poet and story-teller should be put down on paper. The book was eventually published in Arkansas, in an edition of 75 hard-back copies. Carter himself, perhaps noticing the resemblance between his hero and the Eastwood screen persona, sent a copy to Malpaso with an accompanying letter. There Robert Daley read the letter and was impressed; it was "such a reaching-out kind of thing — and it had such a nice feeling to it", Eastwood said later. The letter persuaded Daley to read the book. He liked it, and sent it North to Eastwood at home in Carmel. Eastwood liked it too. They bought the film rights.

Eastwood was doubly fortunate in finding the tale of Josey Wales. For one thing it is a beautiful story in itself, for another it was tailor-made to provide answers to many of the criticisms of his work that have been aired, not least in this book.

The Outlaw Josey Wales is, of course, a western. One, moreover, released in 1976. The connection between the two both creates the political dimension

> **(On hippies): If it pleases them to be hippies I can see nothing wrong there. Each is free as to acts and thoughts. I let people do what they will – 100% freedom**

and places it firmly in the realm of parable. And the parable 'works'. *Josey Wales* is not a 'Republican' or a 'Democrat' western. It does not affirm the beneficence of civilisation, it offers no faith or hope in the workings of Law. Neither is it a Leone-esque western. No Name's answer to universal corruption is escape into a nihilistic isolation, survival through a

JOSEY WALES CONFRONTS THE COMANCHE CHIEF 'TEN BEARS' IN 'THE OUTLAW JOSEY WALES' (1976)

self-awareness that borders on narcissism. He is a fantasy figure — one who says a great deal about what is wrong with society, but nothing at all about how to put it right. Zen bounty-hunting is not guide to 'living', anymore than 'cool' is a positive response to the 1970s. Josey Wales, though a romantic figure, is not a fantastic one. He seeks a positive alternative. Like most of Eastwood's heroes he is caught between jaws of social malignancy; his Bluecoat generals are Harry's mayors and DAs, his Comancheros are Harry's psychotic killers. But unlike No Name who doesn't look for one, and Harry who does, Josey finds an answer. Other people. And not just the girl of the traditional western. Josey's liaison with the granddaughter is overshadowed by the sense of community with which the film ends. The outcasts have found a 'pocket of frontier', in which personal values can be sustained and life shared. A commune, no less.

This affirmation of life changes the complexion of the Eastwood hero-figure. *Josey Wales* begins with the hero being made to pay the full price for his vulnerability. Once the credits have ended he is, understandably, the familiar invulnerable figure, all-powerful and unafraid of death. But there is a difference. Josey Wales is reluctant to risk involvement with other people, not incapable of it. He feels the loss of Jamie, he becomes 'more than a friend' to Lone Watie. Gradually he allows himself to take on more and more responsibilities, and so to become more and more vulnerable. As such his hero persona is much more acceptable; he is not doing it all just for himself. The power and the style of Josey Wales are consequently 'legitimate' spectacle.

No previous Eastwood hero has offered an alternative society as part of his condemnation of the existing system. Rather they have offered a dogged insistence on the right of the individual to shape his own destiny and to live by his own values, and so doomed themselves to isolation, and to wielding their prowess like sharks in a packed swimming pool. In *Josey Wales'* key scene, Josey confronts the Comanche chief Ten Bears. "I come here to die with you, or live with you", he says. "Dyin' ain't hard for people like you and me, it's the livin' that's hard . . . Governments don't live together, people live together." Josey gives Ten Bears his "word of death", his ability and willingness to kill and die, and his "word of life", his ability and willingness to share the land in peace. Ten Bears, seeing that the former is true, knows that the latter is also true. "It shall be life", he says.

Dirty Harry never gets to meet a comparable figure. There would be no point. He has no 'word of life' to offer anyone. Only a personal morality at odds with its social context, a 44 Magnum and its 'word of death'. The main challenge now facing Eastwood is clearly that of creating a contemporary character who is as affirmative as Josey Wales. In such a world this is no easy task. But perhaps it is not beyond him. For over a decade now he has been consistently making films that both entertain and ask relevant questions about the way we live. And that in itself is some achievement.

THE TRAIL OF JOSEY WALES

KANSAS

Osage

Neosho

Oceola Ferry

Josey meets Lone Waite

INDIAN NATIONS

Trading Post

Arkansas

Red

Death of Jamie

Brazos

Towash — Where Josey and Lone kill four soldiers

Colorado

Battle with Commancheros

TEXAS

The dying border town

FILMOGRAPHY

Minor Parts

Revenge of the Creature (1954)
Director: Jack Arnold. Screenplay: Martin Berkeley (from story by William Alland). Producer: Universal-International. Stars: Brett Halsey, John Agar, John Bromfield.

Francis in the Navy (1954)
Director: Arthur Lubin. Screenplay: Devery Freeman. Producer: Universal-International. Stars: Donald O'Connor, Martha Hyer, Jim Backus.

Lady Godiva (1954)
Director: Arthur Lubin. Screenplay: Oscar Brodney, Harry Ruskin (from story by Oscar Brodney). Producer: Universal-International. Stars: Maureen O'Hara, George Nader.

Tarantula (1954)
Director: Jack Arnold. Screenplay: Robert Fresco and Martin Berkeley (from story by Robert Fresco and Jack Arnold). Producer: Universal-International. Stars: Raymond Bailey, John Agar. John Agar.

Never Say Goodbye (1955)
Director: Jerry Hopper. Screenplay: Charles Hoffman. Producer: Jerry Hopper. Stars: Rock Hudson, George Sanders.

The First Travelling Saleslady (1955)
Director: Arthur Lubin. Screenplay: Devery Freeman and Stephen Longstreet. Producer: Arthur Lubin. Stars: Ginger Rogers, Barry Nelson, James Arness, Carol Channing.

Star in the Dust (1955)
Director: Charles Haas. Screenplay: Oscar Brodney. Producer: Universal-International. Stars: John Agar, Mamie Van Doren, Richard Boone.

Escapade in Japan (1956)
Director: Arthur Lubin. Screenplay: Winston Miller. Producer: Arthur Lubin. Stars: Teresa Wright, Cameron Mitchell.

Ambush at Cimarron Pass (1957)
Director: Jodie Copelan. Screenplay: Richard Taylor and John Butler (from story by Robert Reeds and Robert Woods). Producer: Regal (for Twentieth Century-Fox). Stars: Scott Brady, William Vaughan, Keith Richards. This was Eastwood's first major part.

CLINT AT HOME WITH SON KYLE AND DAUGHTER ALISON

Lafayette Escadrille (UK title — Hell Bent for Glory) (1958)
Director: William A. Wellman. Screenplay: A. S. Fleischman (from story by William A. Wellman). Producer: Warner Brothers. Stars: Tab Hunter, Etchika Choureau. Eastwood appeared 8th on the cast list.

Starring Parts

A Fistful of Dollars (1964)
Director: Sergio Leone. Screenplay: Sergio Leone and Duccio Tessari (from story for *Yojimbo* by Akira Kurosawa and Ryuzo Kikushima). Producer: Harry Colombo and George Papi. Co-stars: Gian Maria Volonte (appearing on cast-list as John Wels), Marianne Koch.

For a Few Dollars More (1965)
Director: Sergio Leone. Screenplay: Luciano Vincenzoni (from story by Sergio Leone and Fulvio Morzella). Producer: Alberto Grimaldi. Co-stars: Lee Van Cleef, Gian Maria Volonte.

The Good, The Bad and The Ugly (1966)
Director: Sergio Leone. Screenplay: Age-Scarpelli, Luciano Vincenzoni and Sergio Leone (from story by same three). Producer: Alberto Grimaldi. Co-stars: Eli Wallach, Lee Van Cleef.

The Witches (Le Streghe) (1967)
(5th Section — 'A Night Like Any Other')
Director: Vittorio de Sica. Screenplay: Cesare Zavattini, Fabio Carpi, Enzio Muzil. Producer: Dino de Laurentiis. Co-Star: Sylvana Mangano.

Hang 'Em High (1968)
Director: Ted Post. Screenplay: Leonard Freeman and Mel Goldberg. Producer: Leonard Freeman. Co-stars: Inger Stevens, Ed Begley, Pat Hingle, Arlene Golonka.

Coogan's Bluff (1968)
Director: Don Siegel. Screenplay: Herman Miller, Dean Reisner and Howard Rodman. Producer: Don Siegel. Executive Producer: Richard E. Lyons. Co-stars: Lee J. Cobb, Susan Clark, Tisha Sterling, Don Stroud.

Where Eagles Dare (1969)
Director: Brian G. Hutton. Screenplay: Alistair MacLean (from his own novel). Producer: Elliott Gershwin and Jerry Kastner. Co-stars: Richard Burton, Mary Ure.

Paint Your Wagon (1969)
Director: Joshua Logan. Screenplay: Alan Jay Lerner. Producer: Alan Jay Lerner. Music: Frederick Loewe. Lyrics: Alan Jay Lerner. Co-stars: Lee Marvin, Jean Seberg.

Kelly's Heroes (1970)
Director: Brian G. Hutton. Screenplay: Troy Kennedy Martin. Producer: Gabriel Katzka and Sidney Beckerman. Co-stars: Telly Savalas, Don Rickles, Donald Sutherland, Carol O'Connor.

LOCATIONS FOR EASTWOOD WESTERNS

KEY
1. Fistful of Dollars
2. For a Few Dollars More
3. The Good, The Bad and The Ugly
4. Hang 'em High
5. The Beguiled
6. Joe Kidd
7. High Plains Drifter
8. Paint Your Wagon

SPAIN

3 Nr. Burgos

2 Nr. Madrid

1 2 3 Almeria

USA

8 Oregon

OREGON

7 Mona Lake

6 Nr. Bishop

4 Conejo Valley

CALIFORNIA

NEVADA

UTAH

COLORADO

KANSAS

ARIZONA

NEW MEXICO

OKLAHOMA

ARK

LA

6 Tucson

4 White Sands National Park

4 Rio Grande

The Trail of Josey Wales

5 Nr. New Orleans

TEXAS

Two Mules for Sister Sara (1970)
Director: Don Siegel. Screenplay: Albert Maltz (from story by Budd Boetticher). Producer: Martin Rackin and Carroll Case. Co-star: Shirley MacLaine.

The Beguiled (1971)
Director: Don Siegel. Screenplay: John B. Sherry and Grimes Grice (from novel by Thomas Cullinan). Producer: Don Siegel. Co-stars: Geraldine Page, Elizabeth Hartman.

Play 'Misty' For Me (1971)
Director: Clint Eastwood. Screenplay: Jo Heims and Dean Reisner (from story by Jo Heims). Producer: Robert Daley. Co-stars: Jessica Walters, Donna Mills.

Dirty Harry (1971)
Director: Don Siegel. Screenplay: Harry Julian Fink, R. M. Fink and Dean Reisner. Producer: Don Siegel. Executive Producer: Robert Daley. Co-stars: Harry Guardino, Andy Robinson, Reni Santoni.

Joe Kidd (1972)
Director: John Sturges. Screenplay: Elmore Leonard. Producer: Sidney Beckerman. Executive Producer: Robert Daley. Co-stars: Robert Duval, John Saxon, Don Stroud, Stella Garcia.

High Plains Drifter (1972)
Director: Clint Eastwood. Screenplay: Ernest Tidyman. Producer: Robert Daley. Executive Producer: Jennings Lang. Co-stars: Verna Bloom, Mariana Hill, Billy Curtis, Mitchell Ryan.

Breezy (1973)
Director: Clint Eastwood. Screenplay: Jo Heims. Producer: Robert Daley. Executive Producer: Jennings Lang. Stars: William Holden, Kay Lenz (Eastwood did not appear in the film).

Magnum Force (1973)
Director: Ted Post. Screenplay: John Milius and Michael Cimino (from story by John Milius). Producer: Robert Daley. Co-stars: Hal Holbrook, Felton Perry, Mitchell Ryan, David Soul, Tim Matheson.

Thunderbolt and Lightfoot (1974)
Director: Michael Cimino. Screenplay: Michael Cimino. Producer: Robert Daley. Co-stars: Jeff Bridges, George Kennedy.

The Eiger Sanction (1975)
Director: Clint Eastwood. Screenplay: Warren B. Murphy, Hal Dresner and Rod Whitaker (from novel by Trevanian). Producer: Robert Daley. Executive Producer: Richard D. Zanuck and David Brown. Co-stars: George Kennedy, Vonetta McGee, Jack Cassidy.

The Outlaw Josey Wales (1976)
Director: Clint Eastwood (direction begun by Phil Kaufman). Screenplay: Phil Kaufman and Sonia Chernus (from novel by Forrest Carter). Producer: Robert Daley. Co-stars: Chief Dan George, John Vernon, Bill McKinney, Sam Bottoms, Sandra Locke, Paula Trueman, Geraldine Kearns, Bill Sampson.

The Enforcer (1976)
Director: Jim Fargo. Screenplay: Stirling Silliphant. Producer: Robert Daley. Co-stars: Bradford Dillman, Harry Guardino, John Mitchum, Tyne Daly.

Gauntlet (1977)
Director: Clint Eastwood. Screenplay: Denis Shryack and Michael Butler. Producer: Robert Daley. Co-stars: as yet unannounced (May 1977) — the film is reportedly a contemporary action drama set in the American South-west, and featuring a relationship between a policeman and a prostitute.

THE RISE OF A SUPERSTAR (FOR A FEW DOLLARS MORE)
THE GROWTH OF CLINT EASTWOOD'S ADVANCE ROYALTIES OR GUARANTEED INCOME

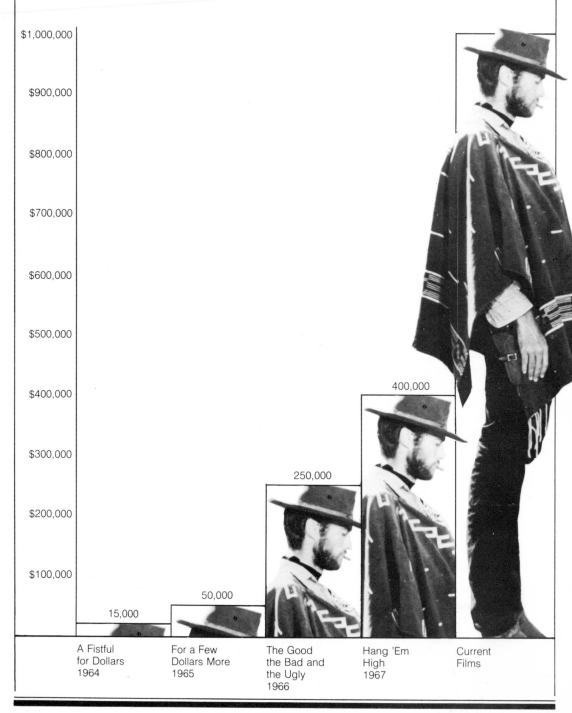

$1,000,000				
$900,000				
$800,000				
$700,000				
$600,000				
$500,000				
$400,000			400,000	
$300,000				
$200,000		250,000		
$100,000	50,000			
15,000				

| A Fistful for Dollars 1964 | For a Few Dollars More 1965 | The Good the Bad and the Ugly 1966 | Hang 'Em High 1967 | Current Films |